MW00529031

"In this volume, John H. V prophets to good effect. While the previous volumes in his Lost World Series are helpful, this one is needed today more than the others, because the prophets are so misunderstood in the church today. His sequential propositional approach is perfect for showing why we so often short-change the prophets by reading them only for eschatology or apologetics. This book offers the church a much-needed corrective in guiding us back to the message of the prophets—a message that still has power to form and transform our lives as readers."

Bill T. Arnold, Paul S. Amos Professor of Old Testament Interpretation at Asbury Theological Seminary

"In this latest addition to the Lost World Series, John H. Walton shares many important and helpful propositions. As followers of this series would expect, he opens up the ancient world of the Bible in ways that challenge popular assumptions about how to read the Prophets, and he also channels many currents of contemporary scholarship in a confessional framework. In the end he redirects the reader's imagination to more carefully considered applications of the prophetic message for our lives today."

John W. Hilber, professor of Old Testament at McMaster Divinity College

"The Lost World Series has done much to help the church recover confidence in biblical interpretation, and reasonableness in articulating belief in the marketplace of ideas. This latest volume is no exception as it takes us back in time to hear afresh the prophets' messages for us that go far beyond messianic fulfillment. Walton's wealth of knowledge of the ancient Near Eastern world brings clarity to these sometimes confusing and cryptic books, enabling faithfulness to the prophetic word in today's world."

Brittany N. Melton, associate professor of Old Testament at Regent College

"John Walton has distinguished himself as one of the foremost interpreters of the Old Testament for the church today. *The Lost World of the Prophets* makes accessible serious biblical scholarship on the cultural context of the Old Testament prophets. This book is a superb guide to reading the message of the prophetic literature with integrity and faithfulness to the God of Israel and Jesus Christ. I am deeply grateful for this outstanding work."

J. Richard Middleton, professor of biblical worldview and exegesis, Northeastern Seminary at Roberts Wesleyan University

THE
LOST
WORLD
OF THE
PROPHETS

OLD TESTAMENT PROPHECY AND
APOCALYPTIC LITERATURE IN
ANCIENT CONTEXT

JOHN H. WALTON

An imprint of InterVarsity Press
Downers Grove, Illinois

InterVarsity Press
P.O. Box 1400 | Downers Grove, IL 60515-1426
ivpress.com | email@ivpress.com

InterVarsity Press® is the publishing division of InterVarsity Christian Fellowship/USA®. For more information, visit intervarsity.org.

All Scripture quotations, unless otherwise indicated, are taken from The Holy Bible, New International Version®, NIV®. Copyright © 1973, 1978, 1984, 2011 by Biblica, Inc.™ Used by permission of Zondervan. All rights reserved worldwide. www.zondervan.com. The "NIV" and "New International Version" are trademarks registered in the United States Patent and Trademark Office by Biblica, Inc.™

The publisher cannot verify the accuracy or functionality of website URLs used in this book beyond the date of publication.

Cover design: David Fassett
Interior design: Daniel van Loon
Images: The Prophet Isaiah, 1511-1512 / Raffaello Sanzio (Raphael) / Basilica di Sant'Agostino / Wikimedia Commons, © Wannasak Saetia / EyeEm / Getty Images, © Nastco / Getty Images, © Micael Malmberg / EyeEm / Getty Images, © xamtiw / Getty Images

ISBN 978-1-5140-0489-0 (print) | ISBN 978-1-5140-0490-6 (digital)

Printed in the United States of America ∞

Library of Congress Cataloging-in-Publication Data
Names: Walton, John H., 1952- author.
Title: The lost world of the prophets : Old Testament prophecy and
   apocalyptic literature in ancient contexts / John H. Walton.
Description: Downers Grove, IL : IVP Academic, [2024] | Series: Lost world
   series | Includes bibliographical references and index.
Identifiers: LCCN 2023037058 (print) | LCCN 2023037059 (ebook) | ISBN
   9781514004890 (print) | ISBN 9781514004906 (digital)
Subjects: LCSH: Bible. Old Testament–Prophecies–History. |
   Prophets–History. | Prophecy–Biblical teaching. | Apocalyptic
   literature–History and criticism. | Bible. Old Testament–Criticism,
   interpretation, etc. | Bible. Prophets–Criticism, interpretation, etc.
Classification: LCC BS1198 .W35 2024 (print) | LCC BS1198 (ebook) | DDC
   224/.06–dc23/eng/20231018
LC record available at https://lccn.loc.gov/2023037058
LC ebook record available at https://lccn.loc.gov/2023037059

29   28   27   26   25   24 | 13   12   11   10   9   8   7   6   5   4   3   2   1

Contents

Acknowledgments

I am grateful to those who have devoted considerable time reading the drafts of this book, primarily my wife, Kim, my colleague at Wheaton Aubrey Buster, and my longtime friend and fellow Old Testament scholar John Hilber. Their insights and suggestions added immeasurably to this book's clarity and substance. I would also like to thank my son J. Harvey Walton for creating the index.

Introduction

When people read the biblical books of the prophets, it is understandable that they are often puzzled. Are the prophets speaking to our modern times? If so, what are they saying? If not, why should I read them? These questions point to an even more fundamental question: How do the books of the prophets function as meaningful Scripture today? To help us answer this question, I contend that there is a "lost world" connected with prophecy that needs to be recovered in order to guard against misunderstanding. Moreover, from observing the many ways that prophetic texts are used and sometimes misused in popular contexts and in churches, I maintain that a book recovering that lost world is needed to discern the purpose of these prophetic books and prevent us from misunderstanding and misuse.

Readers who have previously encountered my Lost World series know that these books address biblical topics that are of current popular (not just academic) interest. The books offer a fresh, close reading of the Old Testament to draw out observations sometimes overlooked or simply not part of popular awareness. This textual work is then supplemented by informed knowledge of the cultural context of the ancient Near Eastern world. The details of interpretation are worked out in accordance with a consistently applied methodology that finds God's authoritative message in the text as being contained in the communication as it was understood by the human instruments (speakers or writers) and their audience(s). In this way these books are working out the principle that the Bible is written for us but not to us. The case is then presented in a series of propositions that move the reader through a logical sequence of the principal points of discussion.[1] A fresh reading of the prophetic books of the Old Testament and a comparison with information from the ancient Near East can potentially provide new avenues of awareness for modern readers that will help them reclaim the message of the prophets for their lives but also serve as a guide for avoiding potential misuse.

What are these areas of potential misuse? Throughout this book, I contend that we esteem too highly our ability to construct the future from the biblical prophets, and in the process the true message of prophecy is lost. In my experience in the church, little attention is given to prophecy, with two notable exceptions. The first and foremost exception is that prophecy is studied with a focus on eschatology—the shape and sequence of the end times. Prophecy conferences promoting such a perspective may not be as common today as they were in the late twentieth century, but they still occur, and the mindset has not changed significantly. People remain interested in the end times as they construct their detailed timelines and systems and argue with those who might construct different timelines or propose different systems.[2] Premillennial constructions vie with amillennial

---

[1]Previous books in the series by John H. Walton include *The Lost World of Genesis One* (Downers Grove, IL: IVP Academic, 2009); *The Lost World of Adam and Eve* (Downers Grove, IL: IVP Academic, 2015); *The Lost World of the Flood*, with Tremper Longman III (Downers Grove, IL: IVP Academic, 2018); *The Lost World of Scripture*, with Brent Sandy (Downers Grove, IL: IVP Academic, 2013); *The Lost World of the Torah*, with J. Harvey Walton (Downers Grove, IL: IVP Academic, 2019); and *The Lost World of the Israelite Conquest*, with J. Harvey Walton (Downers Grove, IL: IVP Academic, 2017). Further discussion of the concept that the Bible has been written for us but not to us can be found in the introductions to those books as well as in John H. Walton, *Old Testament Theology for Christians* (Downers Grove, IL: IVP Academic, 2017), and Walton, *Wisdom for Faithful Reading* (Downers Grove, IL: IVP Academic, 2023).

[2]Even if these interests are diminishing among younger generations, these new generations of readers need to know what to do with prophetic literature.

interpretations. Prophetic and apocalyptic texts remain the centerpiece of such endeavors. I will explore this approach to evaluate its validity.

The second exception that brings prophecy to the attention of churchgoers is when prophecy is used for the purposes of apologetics, most commonly to prove that Jesus is God. Apologetics books offer annotated lists of dozens—or hundreds—of prophecies "fulfilled by Jesus." These passages are enlisted to prove that the Old Testament is the Word of God (knowing the future) and to prove that Jesus should be considered to be God (as the one in whom the prophecies were fulfilled). Admittedly, the New Testament authors themselves use the Old Testament prophets to undergird the identification of Jesus as Messiah. One must ask whether that function, as important as it is, captures fully the intent of prophecy.

Both approaches, eschatology and apologetics, are focused on the issue of fulfillment. In contrast, I find that people have little interest in the contextual message of the prophet; in fact, they may be inclined to think that the fulfillment is the message. This is a serious error that needs to be corrected because when we neglect the message of the text in context, we miss out on God's message for us.

The problem, then, is that people today often fail to understand the role of the prophet, the nature of prophetic literature, and the significance of prophecy. This problem is not just a recent phenomenon; it has beleaguered the church (and Judaism before it) through the centuries. People believe that prophets tell the future and that in the prophecies God has embedded significance beyond the understanding of the prophet and his audience for us to decipher.[3] For some, fulfillment provides the only relevance to prophetic literature. In this sense, they believe that the prophecies are *to us*, not just for us. In this

---

[3] I have chosen to use masculine pronouns since most prophets in Israel were male, and all of the preserved prophetic books are associated with male prophets. Female prophets nonetheless played a significant role, as observed in figures such as Miriam, Deborah, and Huldah.

book, I will be pushing back on that idea as I attempt to understand the context of prophetic and apocalyptic literature and reformulate how we gauge the role of fulfillment as I address how the books of the prophets function as meaningful Scripture today.

TRACKING WITH THE AUTHOR AND ACCOUNTABILITY

As in each of the Lost World books, I need to begin with a description of my approach to the biblical literature. The key to this approach is the conviction that in order to submit ourselves to the authority of Scripture we need to attend to the author's literary intentions. We are not able to read his mind, nor do we seek to apply psychoanalysis. We simply assume that he is a competent communicator capable of effectively conveying literary intentions. If God has used such human beings as instruments of his communication, we gain access to God's message by understanding the author's message. If we seek to be accountable to God, we must do so by being accountable to the human instruments that he has chosen because he has vested them with his authority. If we choose to pursue a meaning that the human instruments had no knowledge of, we would be obliged either to accept that we are pursuing something without authority or to offer an alternative proposal for the source of authority. In other words, if we do not get our interpretation from the author's literary intentions, what is the source, and why should we trust it?[4] If we are not receiving it from the authors of Scripture, in what way are we being faithful readers? Ethical reading respects the author's intentions.

I therefore contend that our accountability to God and the Bible is demonstrated by tracking with the author, to whose message we appeal as the location of authority. We may feel that the Holy Spirit guides us in interpretation, and I do not deny that possibility. But we cannot base our interpretation on the claim that we are tracking with the Holy

---

[4]These issues are treated more extensively in my *Wisdom for Faithful Reading* (Downers Grove, IL: IVP Academic, 2023).

Spirit because that is an untestable appeal to authority for the community. We can claim to be tracking with the author by presenting evidence (linguistic, literary, theological, historical) to substantiate our interpretation. But if we claim to be tracking with the Holy Spirit, what supporting evidence can we offer? Such a claim is unverifiable and unfalsifiable and therefore cannot be evaluated by the community.

If the meaning of a passage cannot be evaluated by the community, it can hold no authority for the community, and interpretation simply becomes a set of one's own private opinions. In ruling out this procedure, I am not imposing limitations on what the Holy Spirit can do; I am proposing limitations on what we can claim that the Holy Spirit has done. When someone claims a message from the Holy Spirit today, they may well be sufficiently convinced that it carries a mandate that they feel compelled to follow. That carries private authority for them, but it carries no communal authority. Only Scripture carries communal authority.[5]

Consequently, my method is going to feature tracking with the author as an expression of accountability to the authority of God's Word. Whatever the author intends carries the authority of God. For our purposes, however, the inverse of that statement may be even more important: if it is acknowledged that the author does *not* intend a particular aspect of the message that we would like to propose, then we must reevaluate whether that aspect can be maintained and why we should consider maintaining it.

Here the reader could well raise the objection that the New Testament authors who deal with prophetic texts do not seem to be constrained by the prophets' knowledge or intentions. I do not disagree. Nevertheless, we must ask what it is that the New Testament authors are doing. Are they purporting to explain the message of the prophet based on what they perceive his intentions to be? I maintain that they are not and will offer a full defense of that in proposition 12.

---

[5]Here I am reflecting Protestant theology; Roman Catholicism would expand authority to the magisterium.

Furthermore, even if they could be understood in that way, that is, using interpretive methods not bound by the prophet's intentions, they have given us no methodological controls that will guide us to safely step away from the author's intentions. When it is clear that the New Testament authors are applying a particular prophetic statement to Jesus, they invite us to consider *their* authorial intention as a new message for the community, not to reinterpret the prophetic passage by imitating their hermeneutic. They also have authorial intention, which is worthy of our attention but arguably does not provide for the derivation of methodological guidelines.[6] How do we avoid opening the door of subjectivity such that anyone could claim anything? Again, these issues will be addressed further in the appropriate propositions.

To understand the message of the prophetic oracles and that of the compiler (when it is not the prophet), we depend on an analysis of context—literary, historical, theological, and cultural—for these hold the evidence that can substantiate interpretive decisions and lead to an understanding of the meaning of the text. For the first three, we attend carefully to the clues in the text. For the cultural context, however, we need to plunge into what is called the "cognitive environment" of the Old Testament—that is, to seek to understand the cultures of the ancient Near East. This is not based on a view that the Old Testament is to be considered merely an ancient piece of literature; it is because the Old Testament is understood best in the context of its world, which is so different from our own. To accomplish this, we must, to the best of our ability, immerse ourselves into what I call the cultural river of the ancient Near East and, to some extent, the Hellenistic world as well.[7]

---

[6]I am grateful to my colleague Aubrey Buster for supplying insight and even some wording in these paragraphs.

[7]"Ancient Near East" refers to the cultures of the Levant and Mesopotamia. It includes the Babylonians, Assyrians, Sumerians, Hittites, Arameans, Phoenicians, Philistines, Canaanites, Amorites, Egyptians, and other smaller polities of that region. It ranges in time through

CULTURAL RIVER

What do I mean by "cultural river"? The currents of a cultural river include politics, religious belief and practice, social norms and conventions, understanding of the world (for example, science), economic systems, philosophical concepts, values, and ways of thinking about the past and about life and death, just to name a few of the more significant categories.

We can begin then by thinking about our own cultural river, in my case, a modern North American one. Here one can see such elements as a strident individualism, a capitalist service economy based on consumerism, an approach to politics based on the values of democracy, a science driven by naturalism and materialism, and an empiricist approach to history. This cultural river is shaped not only by ambitious industry and technology but more specifically by the information available through the internet and the world of social media. Values such as globalism, diversity, and tolerance struggle against the forces of nationalism and racism. The sway of religion is waning, but the culture is still undergirded primarily by the history of Christian influence and augmented by the other monotheistic faiths, Judaism and Islam.

Beyond those values that flow in the North American cultural river, we also tend to organize our understanding of culture in siloed abstractions. We speak of law, politics, history, economics, science, religion, philosophy, metaphysics, morality, and sociology as if they are all distinct. We speak of the separation of church and state and distinguish someone's ethics from their political activity. Such inclinations are characteristic of a North American cultural river but must not be

the third and second millennia and halfway through the first millennium. In one sense, it comes to a close at the fall of Babylon (539 BC). The Persians, characterized by a very different culture, then control the region for two centuries. The Hellenistic period extends from the time of Alexander the Great at the end of the fourth century BC through the rise of Roman control of the region halfway through the first century BC, though its influence continues long after that time.

assumed for an ancient cultural river (or even other current cultural rivers). In the ancient world they have no words for most of those abstractions and would not recognize them as separable.

Such a quick snapshot of a North American cultural river cannot help but be simplistic and reductionistic, but I hope that it is nonetheless sufficient to illustrate the concept. Asian cultures and Hispanic/ Latin cultures might share some of these (independently or under Western influence) but would be characterized by variations and syncretistic manifestations. More importantly, even those who are longtime, fully invested North Americans with shared roots in Western European countries would have mixed feelings about some of these elements. In fact, most people would find that there are important ways in which they disagree with ideas or values that characterize their own cultural river. Nevertheless, we all recognize that since this is the world in which we live, all conversations are oriented to this cultural river, whether supporting it or rejecting it.

The ancient Israelites who were the authors, compilers, editors, and audiences of the Old Testament writings knew nothing of our modern cultural river. Most of the words used above to describe our cultural river (even if translated) would have little meaning to them, and whatever meaning they may have had to them would have been undermined by different definitions. Consequently, though those ancient writers may resonate with the commonalities of human nature that we also share, they could not possibly engage with our cultural river. In the globalism of our modern world, we have had ample opportunity to recognize how difficult it is to engage people even of another modern culture. This is multiplied exponentially when trying to engage with cultures of the past.

If we are truly interested in tracking with the human instruments who produced the Old Testament (and we should be if biblical authority is important to us), we must never entertain the idea that they were writing into our cultural river. We admit that God knows all cultural rivers, but if we were to imagine that he hid meaning in the words of the authors of the Old Testament that were coded for us, we would still be without controls that would help us confidently decode these messages.[8] There is no authority there.

Instead, in this first step in interpretation, we should discard any aspects of our interpretation that assume a focus on our cultural river and seek instead to discover what the messages of the Old Testament authors were to their own audiences in their own cultural river.[9] In the context of this book, then, we need to understand how they thought about prophecy and the literature that derives from it rather than imposing on them our own ideas about prophecy and prophetic literature that are embedded in our cultural river. We need to know how the messages of the prophets were related to the fulfillments that take place. We need to comprehend their ideas concerning God's relationship to time and history. We need to understand the role that prophets played in their cultural river and how God used them in his plans and purposes.[10]

When we track with the authors in their own cultural river, we will understand how their authoritative words from God are relevant to us today. Whatever authority the prophetic words held for the ancient audience, they also hold for us. Whatever aspects would not have been known by the ancient audience should not be foundational in our interpretations. If we desire to submit to the authority of the text, we

---

[8]We would also have to ask whether we believed that God coded in messages to *every* cultural river throughout time—after all, what makes us so special?

[9]Later steps will begin to consider how the message of the prophets can be applied to various other cultural rivers, whether that be the New Testament cultural river or the many diverse cultural rivers that exist today. For more detailed explanation, see Walton, *Wisdom for Faithful Reading*, 185-87.

[10]This book will focus on very specific aspects of the cultural river of the ancient Near East. For a more general treatment of that cultural river, see John H. Walton, *Ancient Near Eastern Thought and the Old Testament*, 2nd ed. (Grand Rapids, MI: Baker Academic, 2018). Chapter-by-chapter treatment of the cultural river that stands as the backdrop to the biblical text is readily accessible in Craig Keener et al., *NIV Cultural Backgrounds Study Bible* (Grand Rapids, MI: Zondervan, 2016).

must act under controls that prevent us from having our own way with it.

As we will learn, prophecy is a well-known institution in the ancient world, and many prophetic oracles are known to us from that time, particularly from Old Babylonian (first half of the second millennium BC) and Neo-Assyrian (middle of the first millennium BC) texts. Even though we will see many ways in which the Israelites saw the institution differently from those around them, their thinking about prophecy is rooted in the ideas circulating in the ancient world, that is, more like that of the people of their time than like the thinking of people in the church today. This is true even though they viewed their God differently from the nations around them, and regardless of the developments that took place in the literary genre as God spoke through his prophets in Israel. I will therefore begin by investigating prophecy as it existed in the ancient world and discuss both the similarities and differences with Israel. We can then proceed to explore our modern ways of thinking about prophecy.

PART 1

ANCIENT
NEAR EAST

Proposition 1

Prophecy Is a Subset of Divination

Readers familiar with the Old Testament will recognize that, in Israel, prophecy was treasured, respected, and a fundamental institution used by Yahweh while divination was suspect and forbidden. It may therefore seem counterintuitive to consider prophecy to be one form of divination. Nevertheless, this association can be affirmed once we recognize that divination, broadly speaking, refers to any means by which humans believed they could receive messages or direction from the gods. Some forms of divination were initiated by humans (pouring oil on water), others by the gods (celestial divination relating to signs in the heavens). Some forms required a human interpreter (dreams) whereas others gave information that did not require mediation (casting lots). Some forms were binary (that is, offering either a "favorable" or "unfavorable" assessment, such as birth omens) while others involved complicated consideration of multiple indications (e.g., extispicy, reading of the entrails of a sacrificed animal).[1] Some divination was formal and involved specialists whereas other forms were informal and could be considered little more than the reflection

---

[1]Excellent introductions to divination can be found in Stefan M. Maul, *The Art of Divination in the Ancient Near East*, trans. Brian McNeil and Alexander Johannes Edmonds (Waco, TX: Baylor University Press, 2018); and Ulla Susanne Koch, *Mesopotamian Divination Texts: Conversing with the Gods* (Münster: Ugarit-Verlag, 2015).

of timeworn superstition. Martti Nissinen, one of the most prominent experts in ancient Near Eastern prophecy, refers to divination and prophecy as both belonging to the category of "mediation of divine knowledge,"[2] which most readers would likely call "revelation."

Everyone in the ancient world felt it was imperative to know what the gods were thinking and doing. Divination was based on the premise that gods communicated with humans through a wide variety of mechanisms. Some of that communication was intentional (for example, divinely given dreams) whereas other forms were more incidental (inherent in the movements of the heavenly bodies) but could nevertheless be discerned by those who knew the secrets to doing so. In the ancient world, the gods could not help but tip their hand in the events that transpired in the world because the ancients believed in the inherent connections between the gods and those events. Other times, the gods could be persuaded to divulge information by being offered something they needed or desired.

Some of the information gleaned from divination and prophecy was considered to be secret knowledge of the gods that could be pried from them. We see this perspective even in the New Testament when Jesus' tormentors blindfold him and then strike him. "They spit in his face and struck him with their fists. Others slapped him and said, 'Prophesy to us, Messiah. Who hit you?'" (Mt 26:67-68). Here the soldiers use the verb *prophesy* not in the expectation of receiving a divine message, or even in reference to telling the future; they are asking Jesus to show access to hidden information. Even Deuteronomy 29:29 refers to the "secret things" that belong to God.[3] As the second part of the verse indicates, however, the focus should be not on what is secret (though such knowledge exists) but on what is revealed.

---

[2]Martti Nissinen, "Prophetic Intermediation in the Ancient Near East," in *The Oxford Handbook of the Prophets*, ed. Caroline Sharp (New York: Oxford University Press, 2016), 5.

[3]This was a significant issue in the ancient world. See Alan Lenzi, *Secrecy and the Gods: Secret Knowledge in Ancient Mesopotamia and Biblical Israel* (Helsinki: Neo-Assyrian Text Corpus Project, 2008).

As mentioned, many forms of divination were forbidden to Israel. They did practice the casting of lots, and they at times received dreams—these were unobjectionable. In contrast, however, forms such as celestial divination and extispicy were censured. Why the distinction? By assessing the categories, I note that the approved forms of divination for Israel fall into two categories:

- those forms initiated by humans but with binary outcomes that are not subject to human mediation or manipulation (casting lots)

- those forms initiated by God in which God provided an interpreter (dreams; see Joseph and Daniel)

Other categories are encumbered with mystical speculation and magical practices, which is what made them unacceptable for Israelites.

Though divination in the ancient Near East was undoubtedly used in popular and informal ways by the general population, only elites would have had access to the specialized literature, information, and personnel to engage in divination formally.[4] Documents show that Neo-Assyrian kings employed many types of divination experts as royal advisers, and a significant percentage of the documents found in Ashurbanipal's library (seventh century BC) relate to divination.[5] From the divination literature that is preserved and the royal correspondence between the king and his advisory staff, it is evident that divination typically focused on legitimation of the king as one who

---

[4]Compare the difference between regular folk today who do their best to do their own tax forms each year in contrast to companies who employ departments full of tax experts.

[5]Sara J. Milstein, *Tracking the Master Scribe* (New York: Oxford University Press, 2016), 10, estimates 25 percent of the 30,000 tablets were related to divination. Since there are many fragments in addition to tablets, some estimates put the total number of texts at fewer than 20,000, but still divination texts are estimated at about one-quarter. More specifically, there are just under 3,600 Babylonian literary and scientific texts in Ashurbanipal's library, of which almost 1,200 are either divination reports or divinatory texts, according to Joachim Schaper, "Prophecy in Israel and Assyria: Are We Comparing Apples and Pears?; The Materiality of Writing and the Avoidance of Parallelomania," in *"Thus Speaks Ishtar of Arbela": Prophecy in Israel, Assyria, and Egypt in the Neo-Assyrian Period*, ed. Robert P. Gordon and Hans M. Barstad (Winona Lake, IN: Eisenbrauns, 2013), 225-38 (231 for statistics).

was sponsored by the gods and was faithfully executing his duties to them. As such, divination often justified a course of action or offered warnings that could steer his policies and decisions.

From this literature we learn that divination generally concerned the present situation and its immediate future rather than the distant future. The king wanted the gods to weigh in on decisions he was making in the present context; he did not expect the omens to tell the future. At times, negative omens would warn of looming danger or jeopardy. These entailed some level of looking at the future or, more precisely, a potential future. We find that ancient peoples thought negative omens could be reversed; they did not present an unavoidable fate. The omens do not claim "X will inevitably happen." They do not even claim that X may or may not happen. Rather they express, with confidence, X will happen unless a course of action can be taken to prevent it.[6] Given such warnings about a potential future, the king would then alter his conduct or decisions in the present. As Michael Hundley says it,

> Omens portended future events by expressing the divine will, which could always be altered by the appropriate human actions. Rather than being exercises in fatalism, omens gave people agency. The gods shared their plans with humans and invited us to shape the future with them.[7]

This is not substantially different from someone hearing a weather report of dangerous driving conditions and therefore deciding to stay home. We might also compare modern warnings of climate change and ecosystem collapse that could lead to a dystopian future (though these typically operate in a longer time frame than divination). The common ground found in a dire weather forecast and a negative omen in the ancient world is the expectation that present behaviors will

---

[6]Francesca Rochberg, *Before Nature* (Chicago: University of Chicago Press, 2016), 247.
[7]Michael B. Hundley, *Yahweh Among the Gods* (Cambridge: Cambridge University, 2022), 59.

change in the hope that negative exigencies can be avoided. To the extent that people consider the future projection to be reliable, they adjust their behavior accordingly.

In this proposition, I have adopted a view, common in academia, that prophecy is a subset of divination.[8] I now turn our attention to that relationship realizing that, if it is so, then many of the above statements about divination are also true of prophecy.

Just as divination involved various approaches to receiving or discerning communication from the gods, prophecy was a means by which God/gods communicated to people. As noted above, some divinatory methods of communication involved human specialists or mediators. Specialists, whether reading the stars or the liver of a sacrificed animal, would use their expertise to interpret the signs and deliver the purported divine messages to the king. Those trained in dream interpretation would supply the meaning of dreams and what response was called for, generally to their royal patrons.[9]

Even though prophecy also functioned through human mediation, the difference is that ancient prophets (biblical or otherwise) were not presenting their messages as an interpretation of signs or omens. Though we know that at times that message was delivered to the prophet through dreams or visions, in prophecy the message was understood to have been received through a cognitive experience. Prophecy is a subset of divination because it is counted among those mediated mechanisms through which the gods communicated. Nevertheless, it is a discrete subset in that it does not require technical skill as is necessary for the interpretation of omens. Prophecy does not involve the manipulation or observation of objects. In contrast, it operates by means of oracular speeches. The distinction is that omens are

---

[8]See a seminal discussion in Anne Marie Kitz, "Prophecy as Divination," *Catholic Biblical Quarterly* 65 (2003): 22-42.
[9]In Mesopotamia it was not believed that all dreams were communications from the gods, but the dreams of kings were considered more likely to be portentous.

observed and need to be interpreted through technical skill; oracular speeches report the intuitive messages received by the human mediator from the divine realm.

Observed omens include movements of the heavenly bodies, behavior of animals, appearances of human or animal miscarriages, configurations of the internal organs of sacrificed animals, and even circumstances such as the color of the city dump. In the Old Testament, people occasionally request omens (rather than just observing them) and interpret them as messages from deity (Gen 24:11-14 [Abraham's servant]; Judg 6:36-40 [Gideon]; 1 Sam 6:7-12 [the Philistines]).

Oracular speeches may result from the interpretation of omens, but prophetic oracles require no such mechanism. Nevertheless, it is undeniable that oracles belong in the category of ways in which communication comes from the divine world. Prophets were at times counted among the council of advisers to kings in the ancient world, just as diviners were. Their value was recognized, and their advice was sought and followed.

Some of the observations I made about divination in general above we can now affirm also about prophecy. This recognition will give us a richer understanding of how prophecy was understood in the ancient world. Like other divination experts, prophets in the ancient world directed their messages primarily to kings. In the Old Testament, this focus is characteristic most observably in the earlier periods (for example, Samuel, Nathan, Elijah, Micaiah, and the hundreds of prophets of Baal in 1 Kings 18), though later prophets such as Isaiah and Jeremiah continued to address kings as well as the general population (more about this in proposition 4).

A more important insight that we glean from the association of prophecy and divination concerns what was believed about them. Like other forms of divination, prophecy had its focus on how people were to act in the present and immediate future. It is reductionistic to think of either prophecy or divination as a means of telling the future; the present was always the focus. The prophets often offered potential futures as they delivered messages warning of coming judgment (such as the message to Nineveh in the book of Jonah). The messages were not designed to tell the future; they were expressions of the plans and purposes of God/the gods (more about this in propositions 3, 5).

We have now learned not only that the prophetic institution was a commonplace in the ancient world but that it was part of a larger enterprise by which it was believed that the gods communicated with humanity. We have therefore learned that Israel was not unique in having prophets, though we will find that Israelite prophecy has some unique elements. It is therefore incumbent on us that we seek to understand the prophetic phenomenon in Israel both in comparison and in contrast to its cousins in the ancient world, as well as in the context of the larger category of divination. Israel was immersed in the cultural river of the ancient world, and if we are going to understand prophecy on their terms, we must take account of the context in which Israelite thoughts and ideas took shape. As always, this approach is not going to assume that the people of Israel thought exactly like their neighbors, but that broader context should stand as the default. That is, if the Bible does not demonstrate a distinctiveness on a particular point, it is more likely that the Israelites thought like those around them more than that they thought like we do; that is, our cultural river is not the default.

Prophets and Prophecy in the Ancient Near East Manifest Similarities and Differences When Compared to Israel

Productive comparison must give attention to both similarities and differences. When comparing cultures, it is a given that as similar as practices might be, each has its own particular slant, but despite those differences, large or small, some common ground can often be found. I will explore first the commonalities and continuities between Israel and the rest of the ancient world, then give attention to those features that distinguish Israelite prophecy.

CONTINUITY

As has been discussed previously, the cultures of the ancient Near East all believed that communication between the divine and human world was at times mediated by select individuals, whom I will broadly designate as prophets.[1] One question that typically stimulates

---

[1]Terminology both within the Hebrew Bible and in the broader ancient Near East is a study all its own and is beneficial, but it will not make a difference for the discussion at hand. Numerous books on prophecy and divination (see the further reading at the back of this book) offer discussions of both the Hebrew and Akkadian terminology. See Ulla Susanne Koch, *Mesopotamian Divination Texts: Conversing with the Gods* (Münster: Ugarit-Verlag, 2015),

our curiosity concerns how the prophets received their messages. Both in Israel and in the rest of the ancient world, occasional textual indications suggest that in some way the prophet had what could be called a seat in the corner of the divine council chamber. In this scenario, the prophet is not involved in the council's deliberations but gets to listen in, thereby becoming informed of the divine actions and plans. Supporting passages in the Old Testament would include prominently Micaiah's vision (1 Kings 22) and Isaiah's throne-room vision where he received his prophetic call (Is 6; cf. Jer 23:18, 22).[2] Yet, at the same time, we have passages such as 2 Samuel 7:3-17, where Nathan offers spontaneous advice to David that would likely have been perceived as a word from the Lord granting permission to build the temple. That is subsequently overturned. Would we then infer that Nathan's presumed access to the divine council would have given him a general sense of the favor that David enjoyed with Yahweh and therefore prompted him to give approval to David's plan? We do not know whether that was the case, so our ability to reconstruct the thinking process that generated the prophecy is limited.

Despite our ignorance concerning exactly how the prophets received the divine message,[3] both in the Old Testament and in the

---

18-23; Martti Nissinen, *Prophets and Prophecy in the Ancient Near East*, 2nd ed., with contributions by C. L. Seow, Robert K. Ritner, and H. Craig Melchert (Atlanta: Society of Biblical Literature, 2019), 5-7; and Nissinen, "Prophetic Intermediation in the Ancient Near East," in *The Oxford Handbook of the Prophets*, ed. Caroline Sharp (New York: Oxford University Press, 2016), 7-8.

[2]Martti Nissinen, *Ancient Prophecy: Near Eastern, Biblical and Greek Perspectives* (Oxford: Oxford University Press, 2017), 184n75, gives examples from Mari and Assyria, and also mentions the Deir 'Alla inscription. Nissinen's extensive article on the subject, "Prophets and the Divine Council," in *Kein Land für sich allein*, ed. Ulrich Hübner and Ernst Axel Knauf-Belleri (Göttingen: Vandenhoeck & Ruprecht, 2002), 4-19, is summarized in Lena-Sofia Tiemeyer, "Were the Neo-Assyrian Prophets Intercessors?," in *"Thus Speaks Ishtar of Arbela": Prophecy in Israel, Assyria, and Egypt in the Neo-Assyrian Period*, ed. Robert P. Gordon and Hans M. Barstad (Winona Lake, IN: Eisenbrauns, 2013), 268-69.

[3]It is clear that some ancient Near Eastern prophets were entranced when they received their messages: "I have become struck like a prophet: What I do not know I bring forth." Nissinen, *Prophets and Prophecy*, 118b.12.

ancient Near East, the resulting oracle often took the form of "thus says [divine name] . . ." to introduce prophetic oracles:

Thus says Adad: "I have given the whole country to Yaḫdun Lim."[4]

Thus says Shamash: "I am the lord of the land."[5]

Thus says Shaushka of Nineveh, the Lady of all countries: "I want to go to Egypt, the country that I love, and then return."[6]

The common ground is that the oracles take the form of direct divine speech. Such prophets are therefore presenting themselves not as simply conveying the gist of what they believe to be the divine will but as relating the very words of the deity. By this very basic observation of continuity, we can see that the Israelites were not under the impression that they were providing something that was unavailable in the rest of the ancient world. The idea that certain humans could speak on behalf of God was a given in their cultural river. It was not the institution that was unique but the nature of the God who spoke.

If the prophets were believed to have access to the divine council and their oracles were accepted as divine words, it is no surprise that in Israel and the rest of the ancient world the prophets had a culturally recognized credibility. In the polytheistic world of the ancient Near East, it did not matter which god a prophet spoke for; the institution was accepted as genuine. This can be compared to how we think about the practice of meteorology today. Different outlets have different meteorologists, but they all are engaged in the same institution and use the same methods. Even though our favorite meteorologist sometimes gets it wrong, that does not lead us to dismiss the institution. We may have some that we trust more than others, but, regardless, the institution has an established cultural credibility.

---

[4]Nissinen, *Prophets and Prophecy*, 21 (2.5-6).
[5]Nissinen, *Prophets and Prophecy*, 24 (4.3).
[6]Nissinen, *Prophets and Prophecy*, 183 (121.13-15).

This would explain, for example, why the king of Nineveh so readily accepts the credibility of Jonah's message. Nevertheless, we also recognize that the Israelites were aware of the disturbing phenomenon of false prophecy. For them, false prophecy was not just about their assessment of messages coming from the prophets of Baal or Asherah—rendered false by virtue of the powerlessness of the god for whom they spoke. More insidiously, the book of Jeremiah makes it plain that his prophetic antagonists are giving messages purportedly from Yahweh that disconcertingly conflict with Jeremiah's messages, and Jeremiah considers this dangerous because of the threat to the inherent credibility of the prophetic institution. His frustration is also exacerbated by the human reality that people are more likely to be willing to credit positive messages (like those given by his opponents) than negative ones (such as those presented by Jeremiah). In the ancient Near East, it is clear that the king's diviners could at times offer conflicting interpretations and differing courses of action.

Given the cultural respect attributed to prophecy (if not always to each prophet), based on the cultural credibility that the prophets enjoyed, it is no surprise that prophetic oracles were desired, respected, and at times feared by kings. Kings and kingdoms could be toppled by the word of the prophet speaking the plan of God. If a prophet indicated that a king had lost the favor of the gods (who put him on the throne), that message could become a neon sign inviting the overthrow of the king (see the scene depicted in 2 Kings 9).

The Neo-Assyrian kings show themselves to have been well aware of how a negative omen or prophecy could undermine their sometimes tenuous grip on the reins of power. This was particularly true of dream interpreters but also extends to other forms of divination.[7] The danger that divination specialists, including prophets, could be supporters of

---

[7]For example, on oil divination, see Stefan M. Maul, *The Art of Divination in the Ancient Near East*, trans. Brian McNeil and Alexander Johannes Edmonds (Waco, TX: Baylor University Press, 2018), 136, 248.

opposing factions and subvert kingship with false divinations was well recognized in the ancient world. Nissinen collects references made to prophecy in Neo-Assyrian texts that testify to this danger: "A slave girl of Bel-ahu-uṣur . . . on the outskirts of Harran; since Sivan (III) she is *enraptured* and speaks a good word about him: 'This is the word of of Nusku: The kingship is for Sasî! I will destroy the name and seed of Sennacherib!'"[8]

In Israel, this reality is confirmed when we see Ahab's fear of Elijah (1 Kings 17–18) and Micaiah (1 Kings 22). The exigency of a coup is explicitly demonstrated in 2 Kings 8:7-15 and 2 Kings 9. Divine condemnation of a king implicitly offered divine support of those overthrowing him. This explains why Samuel's announcement of Saul's loss of Yahweh's favor (1 Sam 13:1-15; 15:1-35) is so devastating. Even though that soon leads to the anointing of David, it is many years until David comes to the throne, and the books of Samuel take great pains to make the case that David's succession was not brought about by coup.

In the ancient world, prophets could serve officially and regularly or unofficially and ad hoc. Many of the prophetic texts from the eighteenth-century BC town of Mari are preserved in letters from regional officials to the king written to report prophetic messages for the king that were conveyed to the officials. The prophets who generated these messages had no official position in the court, and they were not necessarily known as prophets by trade.[9] In Israel, we find both court prophets such as Nathan (under David) or Isaiah (under Hezekiah) and prophets whose roles were unofficial. One example is Elijah, who, though apparently following a calling as a prophet (therefore not ad hoc), was certainly not in the employ of the royal court under Ahab and Jezebel. In the next century, we encounter Amos, who explicitly denied being a formal prophet and had a relatively short time of ministry in that role.

---

[8]Martti Nissinen, *References to Prophecy in Neo-Assyrian Sources*, State Archives of Assyria 7 (Helsinki: Neo-Assyrian Text Corpus Project, 1998), 111 (ll. 2-5). Translated texts are found on 109-15.
[9]Jonathan Stökl, *Prophecy in the Ancient Near East* (Leiden: Brill, 2012), 209-11.

Another aspect that is common ground between the prophets of the ancient Near East and those in Israel is that they share an inherent belief concerning the divine role in events. The gods were considered active and engaged, and Yahweh no less so. Once the premise of such activity is accepted, it becomes imperative to discover the plans and intended actions of the gods. Modern readers recognize that this premise is not generally accepted in our culture. Among Christians, it would be acknowledged, though probably not at such a pervasive level as was believed in the ancient world. Yet this is not an area where Israel's neighbors thought differently, and it is therefore not a presupposition that differentiated the institution and operation of prophecy in Israel from others in their world. What distinction there was became manifest in the question concerning whether there was a larger comprehensive plan that drove the divine engagement.

The involvement of the gods was perhaps nowhere more essentially relevant than in the context of battle. Warfare was an expensive undertaking (in terms of both supplies and human resources) and was inherently risky. Kings therefore wanted to be assured that the gods supported any military activity that they were considering. Many of the prophetic texts from the ancient world give information concerning victory in battle or promising defeat of enemies.[10] So, for example, the god Amun conveys to Ramesses II: "Go forward, I am with you! I am your Father, my hand is in yours!"[11] In fact, kings would be reluctant to go to battle without such approval from the gods. One prophet exhorts the Mari king Zimri-Lim, "If you go off to the war, never do so without consulting an oracle. When I become manifest in my oracle, go to the war. If it does not happen, do not go out of the city gate."[12] As a final example, Ishtar encourages the Assyrian king

---

[10]Charlie Trimm, *Fighting for the King and the Gods: A Survey of Warfare in the Ancient Near East* (Atlanta: SBL Press, 2017), 588-600.

[11]John L. Foster, trans., *Hymns, Prayers, and Songs: An Anthology of Ancient Egyptian Lyric Poetry* (Atlanta: Scholars Press, 1995), 169.

[12]Nissinen, *Prophets and Prophecy*, 22.

Esarhaddon, "I will flay your enemies and deliver them up to you. I am Ishtar of Arbela, I go before you and behind you."[13]

In the Old Testament, prophets also figure or function prominently in the military activities of the Israelites.[14] In Moses' prophetic role, he brought God's word and mediated God's involvement pertaining to victories over Pharaoh (Ex 14–15) and over the Amalekites (Ex 17:8-16). The elders of Israel came to Deborah the prophetess to receive a word from God regarding the Canaanites (Judg 4:1-5).[15] When she gave them God's instruction to engage in battle, her designated general, Barak, insisted that she come with him. This is not a reflection of cowardice on his part—any of the kings and generals in the ancient world would have wanted to have a prophet with them as they went off to fight the battles to which the gods sent them.[16] Since they believed the gods fought the battles, they wanted to have with them someone who could offer continuing communication with the divine realm. Saul depended on Samuel and even tried to consult with him through a necromancer (1 Sam 28) when the prophets failed to give him information (1 Sam 28:6). David sought Yahweh's instructions in battle (2 Sam 5:22-25), and other kings did the same (for example, Ahab and Jehoshaphat, 1 Kings 22). We also learn that Elisha was so effective at giving the king of Israel information about the military activities of the Arameans that the king of Aram sent an army to capture the prophet (2 Kings 6:8-12).

In the later classical period, Isaiah engages with Ahaz concerning his military problems (Is 7), and Jeremiah speaks of the foe from the

---

[13]Nissinen, *Prophets and Prophecy*, 102.

[14]This is true both among the preclassical prophets, those who appear in the earlier narratives (for example, Moses, Deborah, Samuel, Elijah), and among the classical prophets, those whose oracles are collected in biblical books (Isaiah–Malachi). These terms will be discussed in detail in proposition 4.

[15]It is likely that the decisions that the text refers to are decisions concerning what to do about the Canaanite situation rather than solving community problems.

[16]Nissinen, *Prophets and Prophecy*, 152 (104.4), names the prophet attending the king as Ququi.

north coming with devastation (Jer 4). Eventually, Jeremiah tells Judah to ignore the prophets who are proclaiming that the Babylonian threat is over and instead tells them to submit to the king of Babylon and serve Nebuchadnezzar (Jer 27). Many more examples could be gathered, but this is sufficient to confirm that in the ancient Near East and the Old Testament alike the prophets served as advisers regarding military actions.

I conclude this section on continuity by reemphasizing a common perspective about prophecy in both the ancient world and Israel that has already been mentioned and will continue to hold significance throughout this book. All agreed in the ancient world that the exercise of prophetic speech did not serve to tell the future but indicated how the gods were thinking and what they were doing. As kings particularly and eventually the people in general tried to penetrate, or at least discern, the mind and will of the god, they looked to prophets to offer those insights. Our glimpses into the ancient world have provided the basis of making this distinction. These will help us to read the prophetic texts of Scripture more accurately and guide us to think more clearly about the role of biblical prophecy today.

Israelite Distinctiveness

Now that we have explored numerous similarities between Israelite prophecy and that which is found in the ancient Near East, we can turn our attention to the remarkable and important distinctions we find in the Old Testament phenomenon of prophecy. I will begin with some general comments, then move through a few particulars before concluding with some of the more significant, programmatic distinctions.

One observation that immediately distinguishes the prophetic literature in the Old Testament from the prophetic oracles in the ancient Near East is the sheer volume of the material, which is also reflected in the length and sophistication of oracles. In the accumulated exemplars from the ancient world, we have at most a few brief oracles from

the same prophet.[17] These pale in comparison to the hundreds of oracles preserved in Isaiah, Jeremiah, or Ezekiel and are even dwarfed
by some of the shorter books in what we call the Minor Prophets.[18] In
terms of length, most of the prophetic texts from Mari and Assyria
(the two main corpuses from the ancient Near East) are less than thirty
lines, and the longest (Sammetar to Zimri-Lim) is sixty-three lines. In
the Old Testament, only Obadiah is shorter than that.

Related to this observation, I note also that only in the Old Testament do we find oracles not only collected together but assembled
into literary works. Nissinen distinguishes between "written prophecy"
and "literary prophecy." The former is a transcription of a prophetic
utterance for the purpose of preservation in archives or as a surrogate
for the spoken word.[19] In contrast, the latter, literary prophecy, is a
"scribal interpretation of prophecy" for the purposes of "recontextual-
izing in new literary environments," a practice rarely attested in Assyrian practice but characteristic of what we call the prophetic books
of the Old Testament.[20] According to Nissinen, the transition from
oral performances to literary prophecy generally attests to an adaptation of the oracles that transformed them for a later generation.[21]

The next observation to be made concerns the interaction and relationship between prophets and kings. Recalling that the prophetic
institution in the ancient Near East largely functioned to legitimate

---

[17]Here I am referring specifically to the prophetic material. The larger omen literature from
the ancient world is a massive corpus.

[18]"Minor Prophets" is a misnomer and is based on their relative length compared to a book
such as Jeremiah. In fact, there is no reason to think that prophets such as Hosea or Micah
were any less significant in their own day and ministry. From earliest manuscripts, this
group of prophetic books is called "the Book of the Twelve" and was considered to have
been edited together as a single book with a purpose.

[19]Nissinen, "Prophetic Intermediation," 14. For the collection of Neo-Assyrian oracles, see
Beate Pongratz-Leisten, *Religion and Ideology in Assyria* (Berlin: De Gruyter, 2015), 359.
For an example, consider Baruch's transcribing of some of Jeremiah's oracles so that they
could be read before the king (Jer 36).

[20]Nissinen, "Prophetic Intermediation," 14; Nissinen, *Ancient Prophecy*, 22.

[21]Nissinen, *Ancient Prophecy*, 52, 327-30, 352.

the king, it is no surprise that such prophetic oracles were generally favorable toward the king and approved of his proposed plans. On rare occasions, a prophet may rebuke a king and give him instruction to remediate an oversight, but none of the surviving literature suggests a consistent posture of criticism toward the kings.[22]

The situation in the biblical material could hardly be more different. Here a critical posture is not only attested but was common and in fact was the norm. Exceptions such as Samuel or Nathan serving David, Isaiah serving Hezekiah, or Zechariah supporting Zerubbabel provide only occasional punctuation to the litanies of otherwise antagonistic relationships between the prophets and the kings.[23]

Another element pertaining to the prophets' message shifts our attention from having the kings as their target audience to a focus on the broader popular audience that many of the Israelite prophets addressed. In the corpuses of prophetic literature from the ancient world, the prophets' messages that we have were directed almost exclusively to the king and his court.[24] In the preclassical prophecy in Israel, that is also the case, as is evident in the prophetic role played by Samuel, Nathan, and Elijah (unofficially). Collections of prophetic oracles such as those found in Isaiah, Jeremiah, Ezekiel, and the Book of the Twelve reflect, in contrast, a democratization as they find their target in the common people rather than exclusively in the royal court.

Typically in the ancient Near East, the message was directed to the king, and he made decisions in accordance with the messages given

---

[22]This may reflect only that the preserved exemplars are those that have been committed to writing and housed in the royal archives. If there was a strain of prophecy that was critical, it would be no surprise to learn that it was not recorded or preserved.

[23]Examples such as Samuel and Saul, Ahab and Elijah, Jeroboam and Amos, and Jehoiakim and Jeremiah are well known to Bible readers but not exceptional.

[24]Again, this may be because our only repository of prophetic oracles is in royal archives. Nevertheless, we will find that the theological context of the prophetic messages that extended beyond the king in the Old Testament makes it unlikely that we would find similar material promulgated in the ancient Near East. One case of public proclamation in the city gate can be found in Nissinen, *Prophets and Prophecy*, 38 (#16).

by the gods through the prophets. He was accountable and was held responsible for any failure. This is true both of divination in general and of prophecy in particular. The king's response would indicate whether he would receive the favor of the gods. Even though the messages were directed to this individual (the king), they had relevance for the entire community because the entire community was affected by the decisions of the king.

In the Old Testament, the fate of the people remained inevitably linked to the king, yet prophetic messages in the classical period (beginning in the eighth century) began to focus on the corporate community itself rather than exclusively on the one who represented the corporate community (that is, the king). This change is evidenced in a comparison of 2 Kings 14:25-27 and 2 Kings 17:7-23. In the former, God had compassion on the corporate people of Israel because their leadership was unfaithful, which left them rudderless. It specifically indicates that God had not yet sent prophets to the people with their messages of destruction and exile (2 Kings 14:27). In contrast, in 2 Kings 17, referring to a setting less than fifty years later, the author indicates that the people had been duly warned by the prophets: "The Lord warned Israel and Judah through all his prophets and seers, 'Turn from your evil ways. Observe my commands and decrees, in accordance with the entire Law that I commanded your ancestors to obey and that I delivered to you through my servants the prophets'" (2 Kings 17:13).

With this change of audience, the messages also took a new shape. Previously, kings in the ancient Near East were generally given instruction and affirmation. In the preclassical period, kings in Israel and Judah were also addressed in those terms, but those prophecies also featured a higher incidence of indictment and judgment (rare in the prophecy of the ancient Near East).[25] In classical prophecy, the

---

[25]For charts and statistics breaking down the data, see John H. Walton, *Ancient Near Eastern Thought and the Old Testament*, 2nd ed. (Grand Rapids, MI: Baker Academic, 2018), 220-22, 226-27.

indictment and judgment oracles were now focused primarily on the people rather than the king and also began to feature discussion of a future time of restoration.

Without minimizing the importance of the above points of discontinuity, I now turn to the most significant differences. By far the most substantial variable is the connection to the covenant that pervades the institution of classical prophecy in Israel and is totally absent in the ancient Near East. The classical prophets stand as champions of the covenant that God made, initially with Abram (Gen 12; 15) and then with Israel (Ex 19). The prophets' basic function is to urge the people to covenant faithfulness, defined as adhering to the stipulations of the covenant. Indictments generally relate to covenant failure, judgment can often be connected to the covenant curses in Leviticus and Deuteronomy, instruction calls for a return to covenant faithfulness, and the restoration that is proclaimed is a restoration of covenant ideals. The existence and centrality of the covenant therefore lends a unique focus to Israelite prophecy. It is also the most important aspect of prophecy in the Old Testament.

Once we recognize the centrality of the covenant in shaping the institution of prophecy, we can see the transition from prophecy that reflects the belief in a divine *role* in events (common throughout the ancient world, as noted) to that which reflects a divine *plan* founded in the covenant relationship. This is particularly evident in the restoration oracles that look to an undetermined future time after the announced judgment has taken place. In that future time, Yahweh will reestablish the covenant blessings, and Israel will be restored as his covenant people, living in accordance with Torah, enjoying his presence and favor. Ancient Near Eastern prophecies feature no such future anticipation. In that literature, the present king is legitimized as the ideal king, and no future monarch is given precedence. I propose, then, that *it is primarily the existence of the covenant that makes Israelite prophecy different from its counterparts in the ancient world.*

Beyond the plan for future restoration and the portrayal of a certain kind of idealized future, this singular difference, brought on by the covenant, ripples into many other theological issues that become a part of the prophetic messages. Nothing in ancient Near Eastern prophecy is comparable to the theological reflection that accompanies the prophetic oracles or the prophetic literature of the Old Testament. Within the canon of Scripture, the prophets offer profound insights concerning the nature of God. Nothing in the ancient world comes close to the oracles of Amos, punctuated by their hymnic interludes, or Hosea's representation of Yahweh weeping over his unfaithful people. Certainly, one would find no parallel at any level to the oracles found in Isaiah 40–55. Even what seem like almost mundane prophetic works such as Nahum far transcend the prophetic oracles found in the ancient Near East.

Much of Israelite prophecy is engaged in discerning the mind of Yahweh in the context of the covenant. I am suggesting that all classical prophecy is given in the context of the covenant. Its audience is covenant people who are operating in the context of the covenant, and the oracles are related to their role as God's people in the covenant. Here we have just touched some of the high points of contrast, which will be developed further in the propositions that make up the rest of the book.[26]

---

[26]For an excellent summary of the prophetic literature from Mari and a nuanced discussion of the similarities and differences between the Mari corpus and the Bible, see Dominique Charpin, "Prophetism in the Near East According to the Mari Archives," in D. Charpin, *Gods, Kings, and Merchants in Old Babylonian Mesopotamia* (Leuven: Peeters, 2015), 11-58. Most importantly, he suggests that some of the commonly suggested differences between prophecy in the ANE and in the HB are not as different as is generally portrayed.

PART 2

INSTITUTION

Proposition 3

A Prophet Is a Spokesperson for God, Not a Predictor of the Future

Common to the thinking both in the ancient world and in the Old Testament is the understanding that a prophet serves as the spokesperson for the deity.[1] On the surface this not only sounds indisputable but would seem transparent to anyone. Nevertheless, many Bible readers think that prophecy has a more expansive purview. They consider prophets to be individuals who foretell what is to come, predicting the shape of future events. The first job, then, in this section is to qualify that idea with important nuances and perspectives.

I contend that we make a serious mistake when we think of prophecy as *prediction*. This is true, first, because prophecy does not just deal with the future. Instead, analysis shows that prophets offered God's messages concerning the past and the present as much or more than they spoke about the future. Second, they were engaged not in telling the future but in revealing God's plans and purposes (offering

---

[1]The same is true of the ancient Near Eastern designation *apilu* (Akkadian). See Martti Nissinen, *Ancient Prophecy: Near Eastern, Biblical and Greek Perspectives* (Oxford: Oxford University Press, 2017), 35; and Jonathan Stökl, *Prophecy in the Ancient Near East* (Leiden: Brill, 2012), 38-43.

a viewpoint that at times extended into the future).[2] The difference can be appreciated by considering the example of a course syllabus.

When I hand out my course syllabus on the first day of class, I have given the students very specific information about the future. For example, I might indicate that on March 16 we will talk about Isaiah. Despite that specificity, when I do so, I am not engaging in prediction; I am announcing my plan. The odds are good that I will indeed talk about Isaiah on the stated day, but that is because I have developed a plan, am committed to my plan, and am generally in control of my plan.

The idea of the syllabus is not to tell students the future but to help them participate in the course, follow my plan, and hopefully succeed in the course by doing so. Telling the future is not involved, and my syllabus cannot possibly be described as prediction because I am in control of the results. For *prediction* to be a suitable description, I would have to have no role in causation. That is, if I can make something happen, then it would be inaccurate to say that I predicted it.

When we extend this distinction to prophecy, we can immediately see that *prediction* would be an unusable word. The prophet could not be said to predict because he is only passing on God's words—it is not the prophet's idea. Moreover, nothing that God says could legitimately be labeled *prediction* because God is always involved in causation. God is *acting* and consequently cannot be said to predict. As an example, in Daniel 11, the text is not predicting the history of the Hellenistic period. The events listed there are being read out of the Book of Truth (Dan 10:21),[3] which contains the decrees of God. God decrees the course of history; he does not predict the future.

---

[2]See treatment in John H. Walton, *Wisdom for Faithful Reading* (Downers Grove, IL: IVP Academic, 2023), 158-63.

[3]A preferable translation is "reliable document," which is similar to the description used for the Tablets of Destiny in Babylonian literature, where it contains the decrees of the gods.

Another important distinction to be considered is that which exists between telling the future and forecasting future developments. In 2017 Dr. Anthony Fauci, director of the National Institute of Allergy and Infectious Diseases, spoke at Georgetown University. He said that sometime in the coming administration the world would face a serious pandemic—a "surprise outbreak."[4] In 2020, three years later, the world was locked down by the COVID-19 virus. Did he know the future? No, he was working with trends, data, and astute, informed observations. Was he a prophet? We cannot rule out the possibility that he was inadvertently serving as a mouthpiece for God, yet he was unaware of it and did not introduce his message with "thus says the Lord." Nevertheless, prophecies can be uttered without the speaker knowing that that is what they are (Caiaphas in Jn 11:49-51). I am not suggesting that Fauci's words should be considered technically prophetic. Rather, this serves as an example of how an insightful forecaster working with data can anticipate a future scenario.

As another example, in 2019 I was speaking with someone knowledgeable in economics, and they stated with conviction that the stock market was due for a major adjustment. March 2020 saw the NYSE lose 30 percent of its value. There is nothing mystical about these examples, and they do not depend on divine revelation or the work of the Spirit. They reflect accurate assessments based on trends, data, and observation. Nevertheless, examples like these prompt us to ask how much of what the prophets said involved these same sorts of observations and assessments. Couldn't any spiritually aware person look at Israel's unfaithfulness, factor in the covenant curses, observe the threat posed by the Babylonians, and become confident of what the future held?

---

[4] Anthony S. Fauci, "Pandemic Preparedness in the Next Administration," keynote address, Center for Global Health Science & Security, January 10, 2017, https://ghss.georgetown.edu /pandemicprep2017/.

Perhaps they could, but the prophets claim more, and the people credited them with more than just astute human discernment. Though God's revelation to the prophets (and to all those involved in producing Scripture) gave full play to human agency (individual perspectives on events and their own particular style of speaking or writing), prophets claimed a divine prompting, a divine endorsement for what they communicated employing their own agency. They were believed to speak in the Spirit, and that is how they understood their role and how their contemporaries perceived them.

Even when the future that they unfolded could have been derived from and supported by trends, data, and observation, they appealed to an authority outside themselves. Modern forecasters can only appeal to the logic of their data, not to an authority, and several forecasters with the same data can project different future scenarios. The prophets offered a bona fide message from God. That is, prophecy reflected a spectrum of agency, human and divine working in tandem in often undecipherable and undetectable ways to produce divine communication in human garb. These prophets made the radical claim of participating with the Spirit.

The role of the true prophet was to see through divine eyes and speak with a divine voice. The very fact that the exercise of the gift required validation demonstrates that the audience could not consistently verify that there was divine agency from simply listening. At one level, the results would be proof. But the intention of prophecy was not just to prove a particular future outcome; it was to lead the people to repentance and renewed faithfulness. That should have happened out of conviction rather than waiting for the actual future to unfold.[5]

Consequently, even as we accept the premise that they received their message from God, we should nevertheless recognize that their

---

[5]As an analogy, people who forecast ecosystem collapse today are not hoping that everyone will just wait to see whether it happens to be able to say, yes, that person was right. The forecaster wants us to recognize the problem and act *now*!

messages often look more like forecasting than like the pronouncements of an entranced fortuneteller.[6] At the same time, even though
we can identify more of the forecaster in the prophets' role, we are not
therefore reducing the prophets to insightful cultural commentators—
they speak a word from God. Yet, those words are not random factoids
about the future. They logically connect to the covenant and to historical circumstances of the Israelites.

This is true even of the very rare, oddly specific declarations. Let's
consider the three main examples.

1. Josiah (1 Kings 13:2)

In the confrontation between the man of God from Judah and Jeroboam,
king of the newly founded northern kingdom of Israel, the altar associated with the golden calf shrine in Bethel is cursed. But the prophetic
oracle of judgment goes beyond a general pronouncement of doom.
The man of God specifically indicates that a Davidic king *named Josiah*
(who actually came along three centuries later) would be the one to
carry out the destruction—an odd and random detail, unnecessary in
the context, and uncharacteristic of prophetic pronouncements.

This example is complicated by the recognized fact that the books of
Kings were written during the exile—sixty years *after* the reign of Josiah.
That means that by the time of its writing, the work of Josiah was well
known, specifically his destruction of the altar at Bethel (2 Kings 23:15).
Certainly, I acknowledge that God would have known Josiah and the
role he would play even three centuries before his arrival—divine foreknowledge is not in question. The question rather concerns the nature
and focus of prophecy, and on that count this is an outlier.

If we return to the example above concerning Dr. Fauci's
Georgetown address, it would be very easy for someone writing in

---

[6]At one end of the spectrum of agency, there were obvious signs—for example, when the one
prophesying became entranced (1 Sam 19:23-24)—but this is an unusually extreme case
where all human agency was overwhelmed.

2020 or later to report that Fauci had foretold the coming of the coro-
navirus. But of course he had not been that specific. He referred to a
pandemic and to a surprise outbreak. In hindsight, however, it would
make sense if the detail of the name of the virus were specified since
that represented the fulfillment of his ominous words. Though technically inaccurate, that would not be deceptive. We would not flinch at
this connecting of the dots. We have the transcript of his speech to
compare with later reports that are more specific. In the Old Testament, that would not have been the case. I would be inclined to
consider as possible that, in a similar manner, once the specific detail
of Josiah was known, the account of the initial confrontation would
be recorded with that information—connecting the dots. After all, the
power and focus of the prophecy derived not from the identity of the
future king but from the inevitability of the destruction of the altar. I
acknowledge how controversial this may seem, but my point is to raise
the question of oddly detailed information in an account that was
written after those details were known.

2. BETHLEHEM (MIC 5:2)

This verse likewise provides an example of a detail being included in
a prophecy. Here, unlike the last example, a specific identification of a
location, rather than a personal name, is central. This also differs from
the last example in that here the fulfillment takes place long after Micah's prophecies were compiled and therefore is beyond the scope of a
later scribe filling in the details. Here, other factors are at work.

The question we must address concerns the significance of the
detail. In the previous example, the name Josiah was in many ways
random and not necessary for the contextual point to be understood.
Presumably, it could have been any other number of names. There is
nothing special about the name Josiah (as opposed to a name such as
Immanuel). But that is not true of Bethlehem. It could not just as easily
have been Shechem, Shiloh, or Beersheba. Bethlehem, though just a

small town, was at the time of Micah historically significant as the birthplace of David. It was therefore associated with the origin of the Davidic dynasty, from which the ideal king to whom Micah refers would come.

The reference to Bethlehem then carries great significance. It is not just a random factoid. In Micah's time, with the Davidic dynasty having already been in power for centuries, future kings would be expected to be born in Jerusalem. The designation of Bethlehem as the birthplace carries important implications. This future ideal king will indeed be of Davidic lineage, but he also represents a new beginning, with implied discontinuity (by virtue of not being born in Jerusalem). The line does not continue from Jerusalem but begins anew from Bethlehem. Implicitly, this king is not only from the line of David; he is a new David.

If the point of the prophecy is this significance, rather than just a detail of geography, Jesus could have been considered the fulfillment whether he was born in Bethlehem or not since he was identified as a new David. That is, Bethlehem could potentially have been figurative, similar to Babylon in the book of Revelation. Nevertheless, people expected that the Messiah would be born in Bethlehem (Mt 2:3-6), and, as it turns out, a lot of effort assured that Jesus indeed was. My point is that the thrust of the prophecy was not a random geographical factoid but a concept about the nature of this king based on a past detail of history: David was born in Bethlehem, which would therefore be appropriate for the new David. Prophecy is not characterized by offering random specific details.

3. Cyrus (Is 44:28; 45:1)

This example is much more complicated, even as it is an example of a specific factoid included in a prophetic pronouncement. Comparable to Josiah rather than to Bethlehem, this particular name has no innate significance. Nevertheless, as with the example of Josiah, our study is complicated by questions about the compilation of the book of Isaiah. At one level, our questions pertain to when the book as a whole came together.

Traditionally, the eighth-century prophet Isaiah has been considered the individual responsible for all the oracles found in the sixty-six chapters of the biblical book called by his name. Even following that line of thinking, still very popular in traditional interpretation, it does not answer the question of when the book took its literary form. It is now often recognized that the prophets were speakers, not necessarily writers (though this does not rule out the possibility that they could or did write). This is logical in the hearing-dominant culture in which they lived.[7] No evidence suggests that they were the ones who compiled the oracles into the literary works that we now have. Current theory is that the compilation took place by a later generation that was redirecting the significance of prophecies because they had realized the potential application they had for their day (see Is 8:16).[8] That is, they compiled the prophetic oracles because, in their view, they were experiencing what they considered the fulfillment in their time of at least some of these oracles. If this model is true, it may be that the reference to Cyrus should be seen in the same light as suggested above for Josiah—a detail logically supplied once the history had unfolded and the final literary work was compiled.

Nevertheless, as many students of Scripture will be aware, today it is common to believe that the book that we call Isaiah contains not only the oracles of that famous eighth-century prophet but also oracles appended by later, unnamed prophets who were extending Isaiah's prophetic ministry into their contexts using his words and ideas to do so. As those who followed in his footsteps, their oracles

---

[7]See further discussion John H. Walton and D. Brent Sandy, *The Lost World of Scripture* (Downers Grove, IL: IVP Academic, 2013), 60-74.

[8]Nissinen, *Ancient Prophecy*, 22-23. One such option would involve the disciples of the prophets being engaged in that work.

were logically appended to those of the one who blazed the trail that they followed.

For those who adopt this view, the name Cyrus is not a detail added to a less specific oracle of the eighth-century prophet when his oracles were compiled (in or after the time of Cyrus).[9] Rather, Isaiah 40–55 contains the oracles of an unnamed follower who lived in the period of the exile (see Is 40:1-2). By early in the exilic period, Cyrus was already active and a known force in the events of the time. The prophet indicates that he is the chosen one of Yahweh who will do the work of Yahweh. Like Jeremiah's specific identification of Babylon as the foe from the north, this would still be before the fact, but the detail of the king's name would not have been unknown. The point of the prophecy is not to perform the party trick of naming a specific detail in the future but to indicate the way in which political events that were currently unfolding would conclude in light of God's plans and purposes.

I am not here promoting any of these approaches to the book of Isaiah. I am only pointing out that ongoing discussions about the nature and compilation of the book do not fundamentally alter its status as prophecy. Prophecy did not require (or even expect) the provision of particular details centuries in advance.

These three examples, Josiah, Bethlehem, and Cyrus, are the only examples of specific names appearing in prophetic oracles in settings potentially centuries before they would have been historically known. Again, to be clear, I have no reservations that God could do such a thing. The question I raise is whether that sort of thing should define what we believe prophecy characteristically is and does. Even if these three examples are taken as precisely that (regardless of the complexities), they are outliers in the body of prophetic oracles found in the Old Testament.

---

[9]For discussion see Richard S. Hess, *The Old Testament: A Historical, Theological, and Critical Introduction* (Grand Rapids, MI: Baker Academic, 2016), 520-34; Tremper Longman III and Raymond B. Dillard, *An Introduction to the Old Testament* (Grand Rapids, MI: Zondervan, 2006), 303-11; and J. Gordon McConville, *Exploring the Old Testament: A Guide to the Prophets* (Downers Grove, IL: IVP Academic, 2002), 7-12.

Now we can return to the issue raised in this proposition. How exactly should we think about prophets, their role, and the biblical literature that comprises their oracles? I have used the word *spokesperson*, which stands in some degree as a contrast to one who predicts or even to one who simply forecasts. The contrast is not in what it rules out but in the focus of what it communicates. That is, the core nature of prophecy is to be found in that it is communication from God about God's plans and purposes, not by a display of foreknowledge.[10] This understanding encompasses all the relevant corpuses of biblical prophecy, including

- that it can deal with past, present, or future. The prophet's perspective and interpretation of past and present events are just as important as their perspective and interpretation of future events. It is the interpretation of the events, not the fact of them, that carries weight.

- that it is contingent on the covenant.

As I expand the discussion in future propositions, I will suggest that this understanding offers other benefits:

- that it can explain all categories of prophetic messages, including the oracles against the nations; and

- that it can find fulfillment in a wide variety of ways.

---

[10]Accepting, nonetheless, that Yahweh occasionally highlights his foreknowledge (e.g., Is 45:21), still that is not what defines prophecy.

Proposition 4

Prophecy in the Old Testament Is Not Monolithic but Developing

Previous propositions already alluded in passing to the types and periods of prophetic activity, and now we can expand that discussion. Though all prophecy, by definition, entails human instruments speaking on behalf of God, a number of variables are observable in the history of prophecy in Israel. The historical development of prophecy in the Old Testament can be seen to transition from preclassical, to preexilic classical, to postexilic classical, and then to apocalyptic. Recognizing these distinctions will help us avoid the mistake of imposing all characteristics from each period onto all the periods as if they represented the same phenomena. Careful nuancing will help us to recognize the distinct features of each one, which in turn will help us to be better interpreters.

Preclassical prophecy operates from the earliest attestations of prophetic functions in Moses,[1] through the shift that took place as classical prophecy was introduced in the first half of the eighth century BC. This category therefore includes Moses, Miriam, Deborah, Samuel,

---

[1]Abraham is referred to as a prophet (Gen 20:7) but neither engages in prophetic activity nor offers prophetic messages.

Nathan, Gad, Ahijah, Elijah, Elisha, Micaiah, and other unnamed individuals (referred to, for example, in Judg 6:7-10; 1 Sam 2:27-36; 1 Kings 13). In the next category, classical prophets of the preexilic period are well known from the literature that preserves their oracles (Amos, Hosea, Isaiah, Micah, Nahum, Habakkuk, Zephaniah, Jeremiah, and the transitionary figure, Ezekiel) as well as others who are named but whose oracles have not survived in a collection (many listed in the pages of Chronicles, including some of Jeremiah's antagonists, for example, Hananiah). Their earliest attestation is in the first half of the eighth century. In the third category, the postexilic classical prophets are Haggai, Zechariah, Joel, Obadiah, and Malachi. They are first seen in the last quarter of the sixth century and into the fifth century.

The only example of apocalyptic (fully defined, see proposition 14) in the Old Testament is in Daniel. I will investigate there the extent to which apocalyptic should be seen as a category of prophecy. We can now proceed to differentiating between these categories with regard to their respective audiences and messages.

AUDIENCE

The target audience of the preclassical prophets was largely similar to that of prophets throughout the ancient world; that is, they gave their messages to and for the king. Before Israel had kings, prophets were often in a position of political leadership (note especially Moses and Samuel). We can therefore observe that the institution of prophecy grew out of a broader culture and initially took the same shape as is observable in the broader cultural context. This observable development is therefore not unlike that seen regarding sacrifices, temples, priests, and kings, all of which functioned similarly in Israel and the surrounding cultures.

A good case study can be found in the material on Elijah. Even though he stands as an antagonist to Ahab and Jezebel, rather than as an official adviser, he primarily addresses them. Perhaps at one point he might have been an official court prophet; the text does not say. Nevertheless, in the preserved narratives he certainly enjoys no favor or standing in the court, though the royals have reason to fear him. At the same time, we note that he has little interaction with the common people. Some might think that his public address in 1 Kings 18:19-21 stands as an exception, but notice that there he only posed a challenging question, in effect, How long will you sit on the fence? He did not explicitly call the people to Yahweh but simply told them to choose between Yahweh and Baal.[2] He did not indict them, pronounce judgment, or offer instruction. They were simply observers to this face-off between Elijah and the prophets Ahab and Jezebel employed.

In the classical period (beginning in the first half of the eighth century BC), changes took place that began to distinguish the Israelite practice from what can be observed everywhere else, and it constituted a radical departure. The prophets began to address everyone—king and commoners alike, people on the street as well as priests in the temple.[3] This suggests that everyone was now called on to respond; everyone was going to be held accountable. This audience remained the focus not only in the preexilic period but also into the postexilic.

MESSAGE

The change in audience between the preclassical and classical periods was significant enough on its own but pales in comparison to the shift in message, which now became focused primarily on the issue of covenant faithfulness. That which had been the critique of kings in the preclassical period broadened into the critique of the people in the classical period.

---

[2]Arguably, he likely intended for this to challenge them to return to Yahweh, but that is not represented in a prophetic oracle as we might find in later prophets.

[3]Some of the classical prophets continue also to interact with the king (Isaiah, Jeremiah). A prophet such as Huldah (2 Kings 22:14) is only seen interacting with the king, even in the classical period. We do not know whether she had any sort of broader prophetic ministry.

Note that in the preclassical period in Israel the kings came under prophetic condemnation. I have already mentioned Elijah and could also mention Samuel's condemnation of Saul (1 Sam 13; 15) and Nathan's oracle against David (2 Sam 12). Moreover, even in the classical period, when prophets occasionally addressed kings, those kings were rebuked or criticized, in contrast to the affirmations and legitimation that were generally offered the kings in the oracles of the rest of the ancient world. Nevertheless, it is in the classical period that the messages, now given to the people at large, took on an entirely different shape in contrast both to the preclassical period and to the rest of the ancient world.

The focus on covenant violations characterizes much of this new message as negative, though the oracles pertaining to future restoration include a positive counterbalance that provides hope. In the preclassical period, kings such as Saul, David, Ahab, and others were condemned by prophets, but the indictments now proclaimed against the people fall into line with the covenant curses familiar from Leviticus 26 and Deuteronomy 28. This covenant focus is then carried over into the judgments pronounced on the people, again echoing the covenant curses. The people are consequently called to renew their faithfulness to the covenant.

All the oracles in these categories (indictment and judgment) constitute rebuke. It is only in the limited set of restoration oracles (less than 20 percent of all oracular material) that a positive note is found. I would then propose that the primary function of the classical prophets was to rebuke the people, not to announce the future. Their references to a future return and restoration only serve to emphasize that, though Yahweh is disciplining the covenant unfaithfulness of his people, he is not finished with them. He will reestablish the covenant in a future generation.

Consequently, we find that announcements of covenant violation are characteristic of classical prophecy, not preclassical or ancient Near

Eastern prophecy. The threat of invading armies is ubiquitous in classical prophecy but has little role in preclassical or ancient Near Eastern prophecy. We find nothing of a future restoration, a future ideal king, a return to the land, or a time of covenant renewal in the preclassical material, and such would have had no possible place in the context of the ancient Near East. The entire message of these classical prophetic oracles is premised on the covenant.

Moving to the postexilic period, we now note that there was no king, so the messages continued to be addressed to the people as a whole. Condemnation of the people remained a common topic, but now, rather than declaring a coming judgment, the prophets identified some aspect of the current situation (such as a locust plague, Joel 1; cf. Joel 2:12) as judgment for covenant misdeeds. Positive oracles addressed issues of spiritual restoration still to come (they had already returned to the land) and included the successful rebuilding of the temple.

In an additional stage of development, the messages of apocalyptic visions developed into a major category by the Hellenistic period (reflected in many exemplars of Jewish literature). These took on a wholly different focus and will be addressed more specifically below (proposition 14). The most significant new feature is that this literature addressed the flow of God's plans and purposes in the larger sphere of world history rather than being focused on covenant unfaithfulness.

We have now seen how the audience and message underwent significant changes both from the ancient Near Eastern phenomenon and from the preclassical role of the prophets in Israel. Once this development took place in the classical period, it becomes much more difficult to draw meaningful comparisons between the biblical prophets and their counterparts in the ancient world. The covenant had come to dominate and transform the institution and the material that emerged from it.

By virtue of this covenant connection, we have therefore found that, despite general continuity, prophecy is not monolithic throughout

Israel's history, though there are a few basic common denominators. As this study proceeds, I will eventually trace its development from its manifestations in the Old Testament into Second Temple Judaism (from the construction of the temple when the Jews returned from exile to its destruction by the Romans in AD 70) and eventually including the New Testament and beyond (proposition 16), where we will find further points of both continuity and discontinuity as the term *prophet* and its associated practice are repeatedly redefined.

Proposition 5

The Classical Prophets
Are Champions of the Covenant
in Times of Crisis

Since I have previously introduced the covenant orientation to classical prophecy, we can begin to unpack the significance of that singular fact. This is important in that it will dictate to some degree how we understand the relevance of the prophetic material for us today.

When I say that the classical prophets are champions of the covenant, I am simply recognizing the fundamental premise on which their prophetic oracles are based. Throughout the ancient world, prophetic messages called on the audience for response. Since in the ancient world the oracles usually affirmed an action that the king was planning, the response of the king meant proceeding with confidence that the god would bring success. This is particularly true in the Neo-Assyrian corpus. In the Old Babylonian corpus from Mari there are perhaps half a dozen examples where the king is apprised of some neglect of a ritual that he must now perform to regain the favor of the deity.[1]

---

[1]Neo-Assyrian examples can also be found in texts such as Martti Nissinen, *Ancient Prophecy: Near Eastern, Biblical and Greek Perspectives* (Oxford: Oxford University Press, 2017), 121-23 (##87-88).

In classical prophecy, rather than being condemned for neglect of ritual, the people are at times condemned for their overdependence on ritual, generally weighed against their neglect of Torah (see for example Is 1; Jer 7). They may also come under condemnation for lack of quality control in their rituals (Mal 1). As Leviticus makes abundantly clear, covenant faithfulness included ritual performance, but in the ancient Near East ritual performance was the primary responsibility the people had to the gods.[2] In Israel, the people's relationship with Yahweh was not defined primarily by rituals. Instead, the broader parameters of Torah defined what it meant to be in proper relationship with Yahweh.

As covenant champions, the classical prophets were raised up by God to deliver his messages to Israel in light of current events. I infer from the oracles that have been preserved that they played their most important role during times of crisis. The first sequence of classical prophets came as the Assyrian threat was just developing. The threat to the northern kingdom of Israel came earlier than the threat to the southern kingdom of Judah. Hosea and Amos prophesied in the north, and it is easy to see the covenant orientation to their messages. The looming incursion of the Assyrians into the area was identified as God's judgment for covenant violations. In the south, Isaiah and Micah, a few decades later than Amos, in like manner commented on how to interpret the threat of the Assyrians. In both regions, the prophets gave God's assessment of current events. Projections of the future were intended to extend the line of current covenant unfaithfulness to the inevitable future actualization of the covenant curses.

Driven by the revelation given to them by God, the prophets took on a role that we recognize today as culture watchers and social

---

[2]John H. Walton, *Ancient Near Eastern Thought and the Old Testament*, 2nd ed. (Grand Rapids, MI: Baker Academic, 2018), 90-96; and Walton, "The Temple in Context," in *Behind the Scenes of the Old Testament*, ed. Jonathan S. Greer, John W. Hilber, and John H. Walton (Grand Rapids, MI: Baker Academic, 2018), 350-51.

commentators. When threatening circumstances arise, stability and security crumble. During the Russian build-up that preceded the invasion of Ukraine, the world stood watching and wondering how the scenario would end. But Ukrainians could not afford such detachment. Each day brought worries—the growing anxiety both with what was happening and about further terrible consequences. Such scenarios of fear have occurred repeatedly throughout history. This is not dissimilar to the concerns of the Israelites as the Assyrian war machine set its sights on their country. What was going to happen? Would there actually be an invasion? Would their God protect them, or would this be the end? Why was all this happening?

That is what the prophets came to address. They offered Yahweh's word concerning all these questions, but the news was not good. The threat was not going to go away. Their situation was going to get worse rather than better, and their most desperate fears were going to be realized. Moreover, it wasn't the Assyrians who were to blame; Israel was to blame. They had brought it on themselves.

When the prophets announced that the Assyrians were going to overrun the land, overthrow cities, and take people into exile, they were not playing the role of fortunetellers. The people had violated the covenant, and such treachery was going to result in God's action against them as the covenant curses had said. The future judgment that the prophets proclaimed was the inevitable result of Israel's covenant violations. The prophets were given insight into the causes of Yahweh's posture and role in the current events as well as into the eventual outcome.

In troubled times, people like to hear, "It will be okay," and have hope that the threat will not materialize, but the prophets rarely gave such messages. Isaiah 7 is a good example of an exception since there the prophet indicates that the threat against Judah will not materialize (Is 7:7-17). The hope the prophets had to offer did not alleviate the dire circumstances of the present but only offered hope by painting a picture of a future restoration. It will *not* be okay in the foreseeable future, but there is a light at the end of a very long, dark tunnel. The hope that the prophets offered was generally not for deliverance but for eventual restoration *of the covenant.*

Again, I write in the time of a pandemic that drags on. Will we ever return to "normal," or can there only be a "new normal"? Will any such new normal be better than the normal we knew or a mere shadow of it? People have a deep craving to find hope in answers from trusted experts. In the world of the Old Testament, prophets (not scientists or sociologists) were those experts because they spoke for a God who knew, and the covenant was the basis for their declarations.

This scenario of prophets speaking the messages of Yahweh in times of crisis is repeated in the Babylonian period. After over a century of imperialism, the Assyrian Empire deteriorated, and their control of the west, including Israel and Judah, diminished. In the latter part of the seventh century, the Babylonians and the Medes succeeded in overthrowing the long-standing Assyrian control of the region, but was that cause for rejoicing or would it mean one set of tyrants being replaced by another set of tyrants? Maybe the Babylonians would not attempt to exert control over Judah, or maybe they would be worse. While the northern kingdom of Israel had been dismantled and as-similated into the Assyrian Empire, Judah had settled into the role of compliant vassal and escaped the fate of their northern cousins. But just as one form of empire lost its strength, it was replaced by another with its own threat.[3]

As the Assyrian Empire wound down and the Babylonian threat took shape, a new generation of prophets arose to address the contem-porary crisis. Habakkuk, Zephaniah, and Nahum represented the first wave as Assyria waned, then Jeremiah became the major voice re-garding the flowering of the role Babylon would play. The news was not good; Judah would not escape this time.

---

[3]Not unlike the mutations to COVID-19 when the delta variant played out and was replaced by the omicron variant.

Again, the prophets of this period focused on covenant issues. Violations of the covenant were cited (Jer 11:1-10; Hab 1:2-4; Zeph 1:4-6), judgment in line with the covenant curses was pronounced (Jer 25:8-11; Zeph 1:13), instruction was given about returning to covenant faithfulness (Jer 3:12–4:1; Zeph 2:3), and a picture of a future restoration of the people and the covenant was outlined (Jer 31–33; Zeph 3:9-20). As before, all of this was aimed at the present generation to offer Yahweh's perspective, to call the people to respond, and to give them a covenant hope to sustain them even as their country and their capital city, Jerusalem, was ultimately dismantled. No relief from Yahweh was coming to alleviate the crisis. The prophets interpreted the unfolding situation.

In some ways, Ezekiel provided an alternative perspective to this crisis period as his messages were given to the people who, along with him, were taken into exile in 597 BC, a decade before Jerusalem fell. Like Jeremiah in Jerusalem, Ezekiel continued to tell his audience in Babylon that Jerusalem would not be spared—both the city and the temple would be destroyed. He also connected these outcomes to covenant unfaithfulness. He offered no hope for the present but to assert that eventually there would be a new normal and that it would be better than the old normal because the people would be faithful to the restored covenant relationship. Yahweh was acting against them, but that did not mean that he had abandoned them. The canvas of the future was painted in covenant colors. This period was also addressed by Isaiah 40–55 as it offered some perspective on the approaching end of the exile.

In these times of crisis, the prophets also offered messages concerning the enemies of Israel. These are generally designated as "oracles to the nations."[4] The prophets did not travel to these countries to deliver their oracles. The messages were not for the sake of those nations but for the sake of the Israelite audience. In modern times we

---

[4]Major collections can be found in Is 13–23; Jer 46–51; and Ezek 25–32.

might wonder what will eventually happen to some of those nations that we deem as political or economic threats, and Israelites had similar questions, though with a different slate of nations.

In these oracles, the prophets identify wrongdoing and indicate the judgment that will eventually befall each of Israel's enemies. In general, these are intended to show Israel that Yahweh has the larger geopolitical issues well in hand and that his plans and purposes, embodied in the covenant, are going forward apace. The covenant is the centerpiece of God's plans and purposes; it is the neon marquee indicating how he is working in the world. The communication brought by the prophets was important because, as we well know, troubled times bring uncertainty and instability. In such cases we do not need to know precisely how things will play out (in details of the future), but we do need reassurance that the future is firmly under God's dominion—that the world is not spinning out of control. We should also be warned against putting our trust in political alliances.

The third crisis period addressed by the classical prophets is that brought on by the overthrow of the Babylonian Empire by the Persians in what is called the postexilic period. Here, however, the threat was of an entirely different nature, though still deeply intertwined with the covenant.

By the time of the Persians, Judah had already been assimilated into a world empire (Babylon), Jerusalem and the temple had been destroyed, and many people had been killed, with others taken into exile. They were a broken people. Assyrians and Babylonians had made every attempt to assimilate them. The Persians, then, did not pose a threat to their lives, their freedom, or their identity—all of those had already been compromised. In fact, some of those threats were being reversed by the Persians as they allowed the exiles to return to their land and even facilitated the reconstruction of Jerusalem and the temple. So, what was the crisis? It was not a geopolitical crisis posed by threat from an antagonistic regime. Instead, in light of their greatly reduced land, constituted as the province of Yehud, they faced a significant identity crisis.

The hopes that had been envisioned by the prophets of previous crises led the returning Jews to have grand expectations of that ideal new normal where the covenant promises would be fulfilled—in a time of stability and security with a Davidic king on the throne of a nation that would play a dominant role in world politics. All the nations would be blessed through them (Gen 12:3)! Nothing in their current experience resonated with that. They were nothing but a small, backwater province on the edge of a burgeoning empire, which controlled many major aspects of their life and culture. They were free to worship as they chose in their temple, but they had neither king nor autonomy. Nothing about this felt ideal. Who were they? What was Yahweh doing? Was the covenant simply now a thing of the past?

That describes the crisis into which a new generation of prophets stepped to offer Yahweh's perspective. These new prophets made it clear that despite the consequences of covenant unfaithfulness that they had suffered over recent centuries, basic problems remained unresolved. Major failures still required attention. It was not that Yahweh had let them down; they had let him down . . . again. In this postexilic period, prophets did not as often identify troubles to come but asserted that current troubles were the judgment of God (especially evident in Haggai, Joel, and Malachi). Worship of other gods and use of idols were not prominent themes, as they had been before the exile, but the people were still not faithful to God, and the covenant remained in crisis.

This recitation of Israelite history and recognition of the prophets' roles in it offers evidence that the messages of the prophets were not focused on world crises or on some final world crisis.[5] Instead, the prophets arose in times of covenant crises that addressed Israel's

---

[5]Here I bracket out Daniel as a special category—apocalyptic literature—to be discussed in proposition 14.

covenant relationship with Yahweh, and geopolitical events they describe pertain to Israel, even though they involve other countries.[6] When we are committed to reading the prophets in context, we will recognize the difficulty in extending their messages to contexts that they were not addressing, which I will refer to as "adoption and redirection."[7]

This redirection may take the form of believing that events in the prophecies are being fulfilled for those who have adopted them, or perhaps only that the messages of the prophets (e.g., have hope, persevere, repent) are ones they need to heed. When readers decide to adopt those messages into their own historical situations, as has been done throughout history, they interpret the prophecies as pertaining to them. But if fulfillment has arguably already taken place, they can no longer contend that certain events *must* happen for God's word to be fulfilled. Instead, such readers are suggesting that though the prophecies were spoken to and about Israel, they can be productively adopted into the present scenario. As often as readers of the Bible have done this over the centuries, such attempts should be recognized as subjective and speculative, and have often proved fruitless. Such attempts are not interpretation, are not accountable to the prophet's intentions, and cannot be promoted as offering God's word to the generation that makes such associations. Instead, these are the result of imagination and creativity intermixed with hope that whatever the interpreter's current crisis is, it might come to an end. Such hope posited in God's work in the world is not misplaced, but we risk bringing disrepute to the word of God when we pick it up at random to suggest that it speaks what we want to hear.

---

[6]This is even true of the Gog/Magog oracles in Ezekiel 38–39.

[7]It is also sometimes called *appropriation*, but in our time *appropriating* is often perceived negatively, much like *imperialism*, or *confiscation*. I would want to use it in its positive sense, where it adopts a good idea and embraces it, even while perhaps redirecting it to a new situation. But because of the negative connotations it sometimes carries, I will avoid using it.

Proposition 6

Prophecy Takes a Variety
of Different Shapes After
the Old Testament

It is common in both Jewish and Christian circles to propose that prophecy came to an end with Malachi. Rabbinic texts repeatedly adopt this perspective,[1] and Christians are inclined to speak of the four hundred years of (prophetic) silence between Malachi and Jesus.[2] In modern scholarship, it was long thought that prophecy faded away and was replaced by apocalyptic visions. More recently, scholarly opinion has been recognizing the continuing social role of prophecy, even though no collections of oracles have been preserved from the late Persian or Hellenistic periods.

---

[1]Tosefta Sotah 13:3; Jerusalem Talmud Sotah 9.13, 24b; Babylonian Talmud Sanhedrin 11a; Canticles Rabbah 8:9 #3; and Seder Olam Rabbah 30. List collected by Stephen L. Cook, "Prophecy and Apocalyptic," in *The Oxford Handbook of the Prophets*, ed. Caroline Sharp (New York: Oxford University Press, 2016), 68-69. Josephus (*Against Apion*) also asserts that the period of true prophecy stretches from the time of Moses to the time of Artaxerxes. First Maccabees 4:44-47 demonstrates that there was no recognized prophet in Jerusalem at that time but does not go so far as to suggest that prophecy no longer existed. First Maccabees 9:27; 14:41 have also been interpreted to suggest that prophecy had come to a close, but see discussion in John Barton, *Oracles of God: Perceptions of Ancient Prophecy in Israel After the Exile* (New York: Oxford University Press, 1986), 107-8.

[2]This view is ubiquitous (as a Google search will demonstrate) and is even reflected in the common terminology *intertestamental period* to refer to most of the Second Temple period.

Even though the apocalyptic genre rose to greater prominence during this period, the institution of prophecy did not disappear. As Hindy Najman puts it, prophecy "suffers a rupture," but it did not end.[3] Evidence that some Jews considered prophecy to be continuing is found in the prophetic role attributed to the Teacher of Righteousness in the Dead Sea Scrolls.[4] Even though the social role of the prophet may have shifted in Second Temple Judaism, just as it did between preclassical and classical prophecy,[5] and even though we have no collections of oracles from prophets of this period, we cannot conclude that prophecy had ceased[6] or had been replaced by apocalyptic.

Nothing in the New Testament suggests that there had been a centuries-long break in prophetic activity; in fact, just the opposite is true (Mt 11:13; Heb 1:1-2). John the Baptist speaks as a prophet, as do Simeon and Anna (Lk 2:25-38). Zechariah's song (Lk 1:67-79) and Mary's Magnificat (Lk 1:46-55) both reflect a prophetic type of message.[7] Traditionally, the end of prophecy was associated with the supposed closing of the canon. Nevertheless, the evidence of the Dead Sea Scrolls and recent scholarly analysis have demonstrated that though various pieces of literature were being treated as authoritative Scripture, some books were still taking shape, and the canon remained unfixed throughout most of the Second Temple period.[8] The anticipation of

---

[3] Hindy Najman, *Losing the Temple and Recovering the Future: An Analysis of 4 Ezra* (New York: Cambridge University Press, 2014), 4. See also Najman, "The Inheritance of Prophecy in Apocalypse," in *The Oxford Handbook of Apocalyptic Literature*, ed. John J. Collins (New York: Oxford University Press, 2014), 36-51.

[4] Pesher Habakkuk 7:4-5. See Timothy H. Lim, *The Earliest Commentary on the Prophecy of Habakkuk* (Oxford: Oxford University Press, 2020), 100-101.

[5] One could likewise chart differences between preexilic and postexilic classical prophecy.

[6] Barton, *Oracles of God*, 115-16, suggests that the idea that prophecy had ceased did not mean no one was offering oracles any longer but that the "great" prophets were a phenomenon of the past.

[7] Recall how Mary's song is reminiscent of Hannah's song in 1 Sam 2, also generally considered prophetic in nature.

[8] Najman, "Inheritance of Prophecy," 38-40. For a more extensive treatment, see Eugene Ulrich, *The Dead Sea Scrolls and the Developmental Composition of the Bible* (Leiden: Brill, 2015).

one like the prophet Elijah referred to in the closing verses of Malachi did not suggest that there would be an absence of prophetic voices until that time.

The prophetic gift in the New Testament has often been understood to show both continuity and discontinuity with what we have observed in the prophetic books of the Old Testament.[9] We are again reminded that the social role of the prophets, the practice of collecting oracles in literary form, and the understanding of the institution of prophecy had all undergone evolutionary changes several times in history. Najman concludes that though prophecy did not end in the Second Temple period, "discernible trends" can be identified.[10] Nevertheless, in all periods, continuity was found in the understanding that the prophets functioned to give the word of God. Only in one period (classical prophecy) did collections of oracles take their place as Scripture. John Barton explains this idea eloquently.[11]

> The crucial feature is not an absolute dogma that prophecy has decisively ceased, but simply a sense that the prophets of old form a distinctive group, which differs in significant ways from contemporary persons who may resemble them.[12]

The differences can even be seen in the prophetic ministry of Jesus. Jesus was considered a prophet (for example, Mt 16:13-14; Lk 24:19; Acts 3:17-26), speaking the word of God as great teachers would.[13] Barton has identified the growing range of the role of prophets as he indicates that it is found in those who are recognized as having "divinely inspired insight" that may result in

---

[9]For the case that there is no discontinuity, see John W. Hilber, "The Diversity of Old Testament Prophetic Phenomena and New Testament Prophecy," *Westminster Theological Journal* 56, no. 2 (1994): 243-58.

[10]Najman, "Inheritance of Prophecy," 40.

[11]Of course, individual prophetic utterances are scattered throughout both the Old Testament and the New Testament.

[12]Barton, *Oracles of God*, 5.

[13]Barton, *Oracles of God*, 98.

- oracles from God
- dreams/visions from God
- interpretation of sacred books
- spiritual insight into God's plans and God's ways
- mantic (divinatory) wisdom
- mystical wisdom
- mysteries[14]

This sort of list would include the wide range of Old Testament prophecy as well as Hellenistic apocalyptic literature and the role of New Testament characters and expectations. It would explain the eventual designation of all those considered writers of Scripture as prophets, a designation assigned as well to those who exercised the spiritual gift that brings insight into spiritual matters. Nevertheless, this is insufficient to suggest that prophecy as it was perceived in ancient Israel included all of these. Rather, all of these aggregate over time into the understanding of prophecy.

This also alerts us to the fact that what is considered prophecy cannot be limited to the classical prophetic books included in the canon. To be sure, all those books that came to be included in the canon were considered legitimate prophecy. Furthermore, everything that became part of the canon eventually came to be included under the umbrella of prophecy. Nevertheless, prophecy that was deemed legitimate (including many of the sorts listed above) was not thereby automatically considered for inclusion in the canon.

In this regard, it will be helpful to recognize the various identifiable stages, both inside the canon of classical prophets and outside it, in the development of who are called prophets (though in some cases there is overlapping) in various periods.

---

[14]See Barton, *Oracles of God*, 116-30. Many of these are borne out in Second Temple Jewish literature, but see New Testament passages such as Mt 13:17; 26:67-68; Lk 7:39; Jn 4:19; 1 Cor 13:2; 14:37.

1. Preclassical prophets (Deborah, Samuel, Nathan, Elijah, etc.; similar to ancient Near Eastern prophecy)

2. Classical prophets: preexilic (Hosea, Amos, Micah, Nahum, Zephaniah, Isaiah, Jeremiah, Habakkuk, Ezekiel)

3. Classical prophets: postexilic (Joel, Obadiah, Zechariah, Haggai, Malachi)

4. Apocalyptic visionaries (Daniel, book of Enoch, etc.)

5. Second Temple Judaism prophets (Qumran Teacher of Righteousness, Anna, Simeon, John the Baptist, Agabus)

6. Anyone considered to be an author of Scripture who began to be called a prophet sometime in Second Temple Judaism (e.g., David, Solomon)

7. Prophetic interpreters (such as those who wrote the pesher literature in Qumran), who were considered prophets by virtue of their interpretations[15]

8. Those exercising the spiritual gift of prophecy through exhortation in the church and beyond

Each of these definitions was thought to identify legitimate prophetic activities in its own respective period as the terminology grew and adapted over time. Each offers its own vantage point on divinely inspired insight.

---

[15]It is possible that 1 Pet 1:10-12 refers to this stage rather than to the classical prophets since the classical prophets are never shown to be engaged in the activities mentioned in Peter. In contrast, interpretation was one of the main activities of those called prophets in these later periods.

EXCURSUS: FALSE PROPHECY

We know that Yahweh expected his people to recognize false prophecy and to take decisive action to snuff it out (Deut 13:1-5; Jer 23:9-40; 28). We further learn that a false prophet could be identified by the failure of his proclamation to come true (Deut 18:20-22). In Deuteronomy 13, the false prophet is trying to turn the people of Israel away from Yahweh by encouraging them to worship other gods. In contrast, the prophet identified as false in Deuteronomy 18 is speaking in the name of Yahweh. We encounter the former scenario again in the prophets of Baal (1 Kings 18) and in the variety of prophets employed by Ahab (1 Kings 22). We encounter both categories among Jeremiah's contemporaries. Some prophesy in the name of Baal (Jer 23:9-24; note Jer 23:13), whereas others prophesy in the name of Yahweh, though he has not sent them (Jer 23:25-40 speaks in general; Jer 28:1-17 gives the specific example of Hananiah).

Jeremiah's situation potentially makes Deuteronomy 18 problematic. How are the people to recognize that Jeremiah is a true prophet and those like Hananiah are false prophets? Hananiah is prophesying peace in Yahweh's name while Jeremiah is prophesying further judgment. The people are supposed to believe one or the other *now*. They cannot afford to wait to see whether peace or further judgment emerges.

How could a prophecy be determined to be false? As a couple of examples, was Jonah's prophecy of doom on Nineveh false because it did not happen? If one were to reply that his prophecy came true 150 years later (when Nineveh fell in 612 BC), one could never prove that a prophecy is false because someone could always claim that the fulfillment is still coming. Moreover, Jonah had said that Nineveh's doom would come in forty days. Since that apparently did not come true, was his prophecy false? Admittedly, this is not the sort of example that people often think of when they talk about false prophecy—but what makes it different? It shows that our understanding must be more nuanced.[a]

As another example, consider the opening section of the book of Habakkuk. He explicitly expresses concern about continued violence and injustice in Judah—a situation that perhaps he believed was to be punished and or corrected by the Assyrians.[b] But now the Assyrian Empire is diminishing, and in his mind any judgment spoken of by the previous prophets has not come upon Judah. In

response, he receives a new message from God for his time in history, that Judah is going to be judged at the hands of the Babylonians rather than at the hands of the Assyrians. It would have been difficult to anticipate that development based on a reading of the earlier prophets. If oracles are so flexible that fulfillment can so facilely be adjusted from one time to another, how could any prophecy ever be considered false?

We can move beyond this impasse by recalling that prophecies are not about telling the future—they are about the present. In Jeremiah, whether the people are more inclined to accept the validity of the consequences that Jeremiah announces (further destruction) or to accept Hananiah's perspective (no further consequences), the present is the reality they must face. In the present, their conduct is unquestionably in need of correction in order to be faithful to the covenant. That is what is true about the Jeremiah's prophecy and is neglected in Hananiah's. Covenant unfaithfulness in the present is the key issue, whether there will be future consequences or not. Hananiah's message had indicated that within two years Babylon would be broken and Jehoiachin and the other exiles would return; it is an oracle of hope. The people should have sensed the disconnect and should have been able to acknowledge their unfaithfulness to the covenant and correct it.

The function of an oracle of judgment is not to tell the future but to warn of consequences and elicit response. If the people had responded with repentance and the judgment did not come about, it would not change the fact that Jeremiah's indictment was on target and that their repentance was needed and appropriate. Jeremiah reiterates that the true prophet will be recognized when his oracle comes true (Jer 28:9), similar to what is expressed in Deuteronomy 18. Then, however, Jeremiah does something that will not require the audience to wait two years to make up their minds; he indicates that within the year Hananiah will die. That is cited as the indication that Jeremiah is truly speaking the word of Yahweh. We should note, however, that in most prophecies recorded in the Old Testament, the audience was not given the convenience of such a sign of validation. More importantly, Jeremiah identified Hananiah's offense as telling lies (Jer 28:15) and preaching rebellion (Jer 28:16). We can consider those to be the hallmarks of false prophecy.

Hananiah was using his prophetic words to encourage the people to feel secure and to believe that judgment was past and restoration was on its way—presumably indicating that their offenses were a matter of the past. His prophecies allowed them to feel secure in the idea that they were okay—that they had resolved their unfaithfulness. The insidious nature of his lies was found in his attempt to lead the people to complacency about their covenant failures—a fault much worse than the rosy picture of the future he was giving them. Jeremiah, in contrast, was indicating that the judgment had only just begun, and that Israel was rife with covenant offenses that needed to be addressed.

When Deuteronomy 18 indicates that the telling feature is whether the portended future unfolds, it is addressing the connection of the future to the present. If the people are not guilty of unfaithfulness, then the prophet has been lying and the foretold judgment will not materialize. The truth or lie pertains to the people's condition, which is reflected in the shape of the future.

Beate Pongratz-Leisten distinguishes between lies that represent deception and lies that represent evil attempts to undermine someone (libel, slander).[c] The latter are

perceived or construed as acts of rebellion and feature in treaty disloyalty. Breaching a contract was an act of treachery and rebellion. Since the treaties were executed under oath to the gods, violation of the treaty would bring action by the gods. This is precisely what we find in the classical prophets when Israel has violated the covenant. Such concepts are well represented in the Assyrian royal inscriptions about treaty violations.

Since Israel is a vassal to Yahweh, her covenant violations stand as treachery that Yahweh will judge.[d] Hananiah has in effect said that Israel is okay. That constitutes rebellion and treachery because Israel is not okay. Correct projections of the future cannot always be assessed because fulfillment holds numerous alternatives. But identification of flawed behavior is not to be overridden by those who simply tell people what they want to hear. Such false prophecy is treacherous and was recognized as such even by the kings of the ancient Near East. Neither the ancient kings nor the people of Yahweh were to be patronized.

[a]For more detailed investigations, see Richard L. Pratt Jr., "Historical Contingencies and Biblical Predictions," in *The Way of Wisdom*, ed. J. I. Packer and Sven K. Soderlund (Grand Rapids, MI: Zondervan, 2000), 180-203; and Robert B. Chisholm Jr., "When Prophecy Appears to Fail, Check Your Hermeneutic," *Journal of the Evangelical Theological Society* 53, no. 3 (2010): 561-77.

[b]It is easy to see how he would have read the prophecies of Isaiah (particularly Is 7–10) or Micah (particularly Mic 4) as pointing in that direction.

[c]Beate Pongratz-Leisten, "'Lying King' and 'False Prophet': The Intercultural Transfer of a Rhetorical Device Within Ancient Near Eastern Ideologies," in *Ideologies as Intercultural Phenomena*, ed. Antonio Panaino and Giovanni Pettinato (Milano, Italy: Università di Bologna & IsIAO, 2002), 215-44.

[d]Cf. Jer 7:9; Zech 10:2; and the lying spirit sent by Yahweh in 1 Kings 22:22-23, which is to be equated to rebellion and treachery.

PART 3

LITERATURE

Proposition 7

Recognition of the Categories of Prophetic Message Help Us to Be More Informed Readers

Already in previous propositions I have had reason to refer to various types of prophetic messages, and I am now ready to provide a fuller treatment of these literary types. The classification offered here is most descriptive of the literature that emerges from the period of classical prophecy. Nearly all the oracular material in the accumulated books of the classical prophets that make up the canon of the Old Testament/ Hebrew Bible reflects messages of indictment, judgment, instruction, and/or aftermath.[1]

INDICTMENT

As champions of the covenant, the classical prophets gave significant attention to rebuking the Israelites for their covenant failures. Failures ranged from disloyalty to Yahweh and misuse of temple and ritual to failures to maintain justice in society and trusting political alliances.

---

[1]A more detailed list of oracular types is found in David E. Aune, *Prophecy in Early Christianity and the Ancient Mediterranean World* (Grand Rapids, MI: Eerdmans, 1983), 92-97. His categories are judgment, salvation, assurance, admonition, divine self-disclosure, woe, and judicial speech.

Though the indictments may target what we could call sinful behavior, the common denominator is covenant unfaithfulness. These oracles at times referred to past behavior (for example, Hos 11) but even then pertained to continuing problems in the present, the main focus of indictment oracles. The audience at times complained that they were being punished for the sins of their fathers (Jer 31:29-30; Ezek 18:2-4), but the prophets maintained that their generation's own current conduct was cause enough for the judgment. These oracles are important for understanding the nature of prophecy in the classical period. The focus is the present, the context is the covenant, and the expected response is by the people who received the oracle.

JUDGMENT

The highest percentage of oracles fall into the category of announcements of judgment. These can be general statements that correspond to the covenant curses or very specific indications of, for example, who the invader will be (Babylonians, Assyrians) or what they will do (for example, exile, destruction of Jerusalem). Naturally, indictment and judgment are often paired together. Such oracles also show that the message of the prophets was to the contemporary audience. It is a judgment that is to come on them, and it is realistically connected to the current political situation. In some cases, the judgment might be avoided if the people respond, so even though these oracles speak of future events, it is not declaring a predetermined, unavoidable future—these only portray a future that might be, should the people not respond.

INSTRUCTION

This is the category that delineates the expected response to the oracles of indictment and judgment. This category includes all sorts of admonition or exhortation. It includes calls for repentance and often entails returning to Yahweh and his covenant. Micah 6:8 is a good example of instruction that, though not unrelated to the expectations of the Torah, calls on Israel to do justice in general terms. When tallying actual oracles, instruction is the least represented category, though it may be implied in the indictment and judgment oracles. After all, the people were aware of the covenant expectations, so we might infer that they generally did not need to be told what to do. Returning to the Lord is always a good idea for any of God's people at any time, but the context of these messages was more specifically a return to covenant faithfulness.

AFTERMATH

The more common labels for this category are hope, deliverance, restoration, or salvation oracles, and, indeed, those accurately describe a high percentage of the oracles that I have classified in this category. I have chosen this label as a way to include all those other labels since, in the larger scheme, they all represent how the covenant will fare in the *aftermath* of the judgments that have been announced. It is in these oracles that the future is most often mapped out, *but it is a future for Israel in a renewed covenant relationship.* Though most of these oracles contain positive features, occasionally they reflect continuing warfare and struggle (for example, Gog and Magog in Ezek 38–39), another reason to use a more general category label. Less than 20 percent of oracles can be categorized as aftermath.

APOCALYPTIC LITERATURE AND THE CATEGORIES

The four categories outlined above have been drawn from an investigation of the messages of the classical prophets. They are represented in both the preexilic period and the postexilic period, though in the latter the indictments take on a different focus and the judgments are seen as more present than future. The next question to address is how these are represented in apocalyptic literature.

In the book of Daniel, there are no new indictments on the Jews, though the indictments previously given by the prophets still stand

and the Jews are still considered under judgment (Dan 9). But the new troubles they face (either in the court tales or the visions) are not presented as judgment coming upon them. Instruction does not pertain to repentance (though Daniel does repent on their behalf); rather, it calls them to understand how God is working and to persevere through the time of troubles.

Aftermath may be the most prominent of the four categories in apocalyptic, yet even that takes on an entirely different focus in this literature. Here the messages do not address what will take place after judgment. And the book offers little hope of an imminent improvement in the people's lived circumstances but consistently presents the idea that the kingdom of God will eventually come and will prevail over the empires. Restoration is in process but is not detailed and is still far from complete. Instead, the restoration coincides with the coming kingdom of God. This idea has expanded beyond what happens in the little strip of land alongside the eastern edge of the Mediterranean to a worldwide phenomenon. In this, Israel is not just recovering from the barrages of empires, but empires are being overcome and replaced by the kingdom of God.

In all of this, the covenant is backgrounded rather than being the focus of the visions or their message, as it had been in the classical period. Here, the covenant provides the set, in contrast to the action, on the stage. Though the covenant still stands as the scaffolding, that is not what these visions are about, unlike what we found in the classical prophets. These visions are about empire and the kingdom of God, not about faithfulness to the covenant, though the covenant is still assumed. I would suggest that classical prophecy aftermath oracles and apocalyptic visions have in common that they both deal with the future shape of things, though each does so in its own way. I will treat the continuity and discontinuity between classical prophecy and apocalyptic in propositions 14-16.

The category of aftermath is the one that often proves of most interest to interpreters who want to repackage prophetic oracles for their own time, and that is no surprise. The question remains how that process can take place under careful methodological controls. This leads us to ask how we ought to be guided in the act of repackaging. If the prophet's message carries the authority of Scripture, his intentions must be respected. If the repackaging, by definition, seeks to extend the prophet's message beyond what he could possibly have known, can that new perspective reflect authority? If so, how? If not, then how and why does it carry significance? These issues will be addressed in part four on methodology (propositions 10-13).

We have seen that it would be shortsighted at best and misguided at worst to think of the role and message of the prophets as telling the future. Instead, the prophets are grounding the hope of the people in Yahweh's benevolent plans and purposes for his people going forward. The four categories of prophetic oracle that I have identified pertain most to the prophet's present: things Israel was doing wrong; what the inevitable consequences would be, tied to the very near future; what they ought to do in response; and why they should still have hope. Every aspect of that message is related to the covenant and is designed to help Israel understand how Yahweh is working out his plans and purposes. When it deals with the future, it is more concerned with *their* future, not ours.

Yet, we acknowledge that some prophecies are identified as being fulfilled in times quite distant from that of the prophet and his audience and in ways that are beyond the scope of his knowledge. This dynamic nature of prophecy cannot be ignored but must be treated carefully. How can we respect the authoritative message of the prophet yet also recognize the varied ways in which adoption, adaptation, redirection, repackaging, transformation, and fulfillment can take place? This also will be addressed in part four (propositions 10-13).

Proposition 8

Prophets Were Typically
Not Authors

Now we are ready to discuss in greater detail the relationship of the prophets to the books that bear their names. I begin this discussion with the observation made by Martti Nissinen and introduced in proposition two that the impetus for collecting the prophetic oracles, originally delivered orally, occurred when they were adopted (and often recontextualized) by later generations.[1] This is a logical enough proposal, but it is difficult to substantiate and is contrary to traditional presuppositions, which have often assumed that the prophets were the authors of their collected works.

Eric Tully delineates seven stages in the movement from prophetic word to prophetic book.[2] He identifies these stages as

1. prophetic event (the message coming to the prophet through word or vision)

2. rhetorical event (delivering the message to an audience)

---

[1]Martti Nissinen, *Ancient Prophecy: Near Eastern, Biblical, and Greek Perspectives* (Oxford: Oxford University Press, 2017), 52, 327-30, 352.

[2]Eric J. Tully, *Reading the Prophets as Christian Scripture* (Grand Rapids, MI: Baker Academic, 2022), 134-40. See also Karel van der Toorn, *Scribal Culture and the Making of the Hebrew Bible* (Cambridge, MA: Harvard University Press, 2007), 178-88.

3. transcriptional event (reducing the message content to writing)

4. compilation event (gathering the various written oracles together by temple officials, scribes, or followers/sympathizers[3])

5. narratorial event (setting the oracles in a narrative context)

6. editorial event (producing the book as we know it, combining oracles and narratives)

7. nominal event (providing a superscription to identify the prophet and the setting)

This provides a helpful recognition of steps that must take place moving from prophet to complete book. If we were to move an additional step from book to Scripture, we would have to add canonization as an eighth step.

In an unnuanced view, based only on modern perspectives of literary production, it would be easy for someone to think that the prophet himself was responsible for most if not all these steps, but such a conclusion is unwarranted (though see the exceptional case of Jer 36). Tully helpfully offers evidence that the prophets themselves may have occasionally been involved at least in part in stages three and four (writing and compilation), though lack of evidence prevents us from extrapolating those isolated instances to all prophets throughout the corpus. From the standpoint of divine inspiration, the prophet is not the only one endowed with the Spirit (2 Pet 1:21); every stage up through the final written product is part of the inspiration process (2 Tim 3:16) regardless of who was involved or when it took place.

Regarding step three (transcription), a handful of examples suggest that some prophetic messages were delivered in writing (Is 8:1; Jer 29:1; Hab 2:2),[4] but the distinctiveness of these scenarios indicates that was

---

[3]Van der Toorn, *Scribal Culture*, 184.
[4]Van der Toorn, *Scribal Culture*, 179-80.

the exception rather than the rule. In reference to the preexilic prophets, van der Toorn notes,

> Their purpose in writing, however, was confined to communicating a message to their contemporaries. They resorted to the written word when they judged an oral delivery less apt to reach their intended audience. Not a single time, though, did they write in view of preserving the words for future generations. Yet this was precisely the purpose of the prophetic collections as we know them from the Hebrew Bible. The books of the prophets were composed for an audience that would consult them after the prophets had gone.[5]

Regarding step four (compilation), a few examples can be found in the ancient world that suggest prophetic oracles were gathered together and committed to writing even in the first half of the first millennium. Van der Toorn considers the Balaam text of Deir 'Alla to offer such evidence.[6] Additional evidence comes from the Neo-Assyrian archives. Van der Toorn summarizes the significance:

> [The evidence] shows that scribes of the temple administration kept a written record of the individual oracles pronounced in the temple, and second, it attests to the custom of collecting prophecies on larger tablets for future consultation.[7]

These, however, reflect only the first stage of written preservation and collection, though perhaps other steps would have developed had the Neo-Assyrian Empire survived. Regardless, they do not yet attest the broader accumulation into literary works like the books of the prophets (steps five and six).

This brings us back to Nissinen's proposal that though the prophets appear to have had occasional involvement in transcription (stage three),

---

[5]Van der Toorn, *Scribal Culture*, 182.
[6]Van der Toorn, *Scribal Culture*, 175-76.
[7]Van der Toorn, *Scribal Culture*, 178.

the remaining stages did not involve them. We have the logical problem that it is difficult to prove that they were not involved; we can only note the lack of evidence that they were. This lack of evidence, coupled with our awareness that gathering oral proclamations into text was not a common procedure in the ancient world, leads me to propose a default position that, unless evidence shows otherwise, caution would encourage us to leave the question open.

With this set of presuppositions in mind, I can at least hypothetically pose the question: If the prophets themselves did not compile their oracles into the books that we have, who would have done so and why? Nissinen's proposal that the oracles may have been gathered together by later generations who either (1) had now seen enough of the prophecies of judgment fulfilled that they had become convinced of the prophet's legitimacy[8] or (2) recognized that potential fulfillment of aftermath oracles in their own contemporary circumstances had sufficient merit to warrant further consideration. We are aware that prophets were evaluated according to these criteria by later generations. The first option is evidenced in part in the Old Testament itself when the elders defended Jeremiah's oracles concerning the destruction of Jerusalem by citing Micah's similar oracles dating a century earlier (Jer 26:18). Though this does not demonstrate that Micah's oracles had been gathered into a written collection, it does show that the elders were aware of those prophecies long after the death of the prophet.

The second option is given evidence in the Qumran community (second century BC) as their own adaptations reflected the oracles of Isaiah and Habakkuk as well as the visions of Daniel, all of which they considered to pertain to their community and its circumstances. Again, however, the caveat remains that this does not suggest that members of the Qumran community were the first to gather the written oracles together. They were aware of such collected works of

---

[8]This could have begun as early as the exilic period. See discussion in van der Toorn, *Scribal Culture*, 175.

the prophets and recopied them, but there is no reason to believe that
they were the first to do so.

When we are pushed to look earlier than the second century for evidence, we are hampered by the lack of manuscripts. One available re-
course is examination of the variant editions of the book of Jeremiah
that are attested in the Hebrew Masoretic text vis-à-vis the Greek translation known as the Septuagint, translated in Alexandria, Egypt. The
similarities between them suggest that a common corpus was available
to both the Jewish communities in Egypt and those in Israel and the
diaspora (particularly in Babylon). Nevertheless, the *differences* suggest
that the book had only achieved its final editing separately in each of
the respective locations, resulting in somewhat different versions. For
Jeremiah, at least, this suggests that some gathering of the material had
taken place by the fifth century BC but was finalized later.[9] In such a
scenario, it would be in the Persian period and perhaps the early Hellenistic period that the bulk of the collecting was taking place.[10] This
generally coincides with Eugene Ulrich's conclusion:

> The combined evidence of the scriptural scrolls [from Qumran
> and Masada] and the way they are used indicates that the canon
> was not yet formed during the Qumran period, though there is
> solid evidence that there was a widespread conception of a col-
> lection of books—"The Law and the Prophets" (the latter term
> not fully defined)—and that this collection was viewed as au-
> thoritative Scripture with God as its inspiration.[11]

For our discussion, it does not matter who put the collections together and when. It is enough for us to recognize that it was likely not

---

[9]For a way forward to account for this within an evangelical paradigm, see Bruce K. Waltke,
"Aims of Old Testament Criticism," *Westminster Theological Journal* 51, no. 1 (1989): 93-108;
see also Eugene Ulrich, *The Dead Sea Scrolls and the Developmental Composition of the
Bible* (Leiden: Brill, 2015), 141-50.

[10]Van der Toorn, *Scribal Culture*, 173.

[11]Ulrich, *Dead Sea Scrolls*, 311.

the prophet himself but later interested parties (compare Hezekiah's men compiling some of the Proverbs, Prov 25:1). We can only speculate what prompted them to do so, and the two motivations mentioned earlier (either judgment or aftermath oracles being fulfilled) remain the most likely explanations.

For argument's sake, what would the acceptance of such a working hypothesis tell us that would help us as we seek to interpret the prophets? First, I should note that it would neither undermine the prophetic books as Scripture nor compromise the seminal role of the prophet as the one through whom the word of God came. Second, however, it would expand the scope of inspiration (remember: *inspiration* is descriptive of the character of the *written* word of God) beyond whatever the prophet did, to the work of those who participated in compiling the book.

In conclusion, what I have discussed in this proposal cautions us against a number of presuppositions that could easily be held. Specifically, if the prophets are not themselves necessarily the compilers of the books in their final form (and generally not likely to be so), we should be willing to recognize the possibility of accumulated layers in a book, as well as contemplate the possibility that the literary intentions of the prophetic book might be considered in light of later compilers who adapted and recontextualized the books for their own time.

Proposition 9

The Implied Audience
of the Prophetic Books Is Not
Necessarily the Audience of the Prophet

The term *implied audience* refers to the audience whom the author is imagining as the recipients of the message that he is presenting. For example, the oracles against the nations that I mentioned previously are spoken to each of the individual nations (e.g., Moab, Babylon, Tyre), but the implied audience is Israel. The prophet does not expect that the nations who are addressed will ever hear his prophetic message.

Alternatively, a prophet may knowingly address his contemporary audience with a message that is actually intended for a future generation. There is much debate over whether this happens, but its possibility has spawned a long-standing debate over whether some of the prophetic books supplement the initial words of a prophet with prophecies in the same vein that are given to later generations. We can consider this using the book of Isaiah as an example.

Until relatively recent times, it was believed that the sixty-six-chapter book of Isaiah as we have it in our Bibles was to be attributed in its entirety to the eighth-century prophet Isaiah son of Amoz. Yet at the same time, it was acknowledged that Isaiah 40–55 was addressed to the exiles, and Isaiah 56–66 was addressed to an audience in the postexilic period. In this traditional model, the single prophetic voice, Isaiah son of Amoz, addressed different implied audiences in different parts of the book. He had been given from God messages not only for his own contemporary audience but also for the exiles (Is 40–55) and for those who returned from the exile (Is 56–66). Though all the messages were intended to inform his contemporaries, he has other implied audiences.

An alternative understanding of this variation in addressees is that instead of reflecting numerous implied audiences for Isaiah son of Amoz, other (unnamed) prophetic voices, centuries down the road, sought to extend the reach of Isaiah's messages to their own generations.[1] They identified closely with Isaiah and even made intentional use of his themes and vocabulary since they viewed themselves as his successors. In this scenario, Isaiah son of Amoz does not have a future implied audience different from his own contemporary audience. He would not be considered the speaking prophet in Isaiah 40–66. Rather, the power of his prophetic message spawned (unbeknown to him) a succession of prophets who extended his prophetic reach by adding their voices to his, also under the power of divine inspiration.[2] Though their messages can be distinguished from those of Isaiah son of Amoz, they are also in many ways derivative. In this view, it is intentional and not surprising that these successive prophetic voices became attached (canonically) to Isaiah, the fountainhead whose influence pervades the entire stream of tradition. Yet, at the same time, they had their own

---

[1]Those who hold this view point out that accumulated layers of oracles by Isaiah son of Amoz are identified as coming from him (Is 1:1; 2:1; 13:1), suggesting that those indeed represent layers. No such identification is offered by the text for Is 40–55 or Is 56–66. Whether this indicates anonymous voices that are meant to be extensions of Isaiah's voice or Isaiah's continuing voice that needs no repeated identification continues to be debated.

[2]Some have considered these to be Isaiah's disciples (Is 8:16) or have proposed a school of followers that grew in the centuries following the prophet's life. These are both interesting ideas but are debated and unsubstantiated. I am not here assuming either of these models.

implied audiences, which were not the same as that addressed by
Isaiah son of Amoz.

Those who hold this latter position maintain that if, as generally
seems to be true, the prophets are interested in generating response
from their contemporary audience—that is, speaking about the past
and the near future with an eye on the present—then projection to an
implied audience in the distant future would seem superfluous at best,
vacuous at worst. Yet some scholars still defend such a distant focus as
relevant to the contemporary audience. For example, John Oswalt indicates that the message of Isaiah 40–55 to the eighth-century audience
is an affirmation of the uniqueness of Yahweh and his intentions to
restore the people in the future.[3]

We have discussed two alternatives: (1) implied audience in the far
future, e.g., Isaiah son of Amoz talking to an audience hundreds of
years in the future, or (2) supplemental prophetic voices from different
times addressing distinct implied audiences gathered under the aegis
of a great prophetic figure. A third view adopts the idea that the book
has multiple horizons.[4] Any of these hypotheses could be defended in
a framework of biblical authority, and this is not the place to try to sort
them out. My interest here is in the question of implied audience. If
the book of Isaiah represents an accumulation of derivative prophetic
voices, it would mean that the *book* has an implied audience that is
different from that of the prophet himself. The implied audience of the
book would be in that time when the book was finalized with its complete set of voices. This would be different from the implied audience
of Isaiah son of Amoz and even different from the that of the prophet
referred to as Second Isaiah purportedly reflected in Isaiah 40–55.

Theoretically, if the book were compiled after the time of Third
Isaiah (Is 56–66), then the implied audience of the *book* (as opposed

---

[3]John N. Oswalt, *The Book of Isaiah: Chapters 40–66* (Grand Rapids, MI: Eerdmans, 1998), 8.
[4]For example, Christopher R. Seitz, *Prophecy and Hermeneutics: Toward a New Introduction to the Prophets* (Grand Rapids, MI: Baker Academic, 2007).

to that of the prophet) in its complex entirety would be the contemporary audience of the time in which it was finally compiled. The generation that pulled the book together, which may or may not be the one that is contemporary with the last voice in the book, would be the audience of the book implied by the compiler, even though that generation may not be the implied author of any of the prophetic voices in the book. The book, in this case, comes together in an act of redirection of the message to a later generation.

This same issue is at play in the book of Daniel. In the traditional view, the book of Daniel begins with what are known as the court tales—narratives about the experiences of Jewish exiles, Daniel and his friends, in the court of the Babylonian king Nebuchadnezzar. The latter part of the book, now apocalyptic rather than narrative, recounts the visions of that same Daniel as he gazes into the distant future—eventually, and primarily, into the Hellenistic period and the persecution of the Jews under Antiochus IV Epiphanes. That is the view that sees the visionary Daniel as having an implied audience in the remote future.

An alternative view of Daniel has suggested that the book is a product of remembered stories about Daniel, adopted by later generations who extend his repertoire to address their own times. Originally, this later generation was posited as the one who was suffering under the second-century BC persecution. More recently, the book has been seen as a series of accumulated visions representing successive generations from the late Persian period, through the early Hellenistic period, and only eventually landing in the time of Antiochus IV on the eve of the Maccabean revolt. In this understanding, each segment of the book of Daniel (for example, Dan 8) has its own implied audience, but only once the last voice has spoken (Dan 10–12) and all the parts are compiled into the book do we learn about the implied audience of the complete book. In this view, as each new layer (each divinely inspired) is added as an extension of the voice of Daniel, the previous work is being contextualized for a new generation. They may be asking, for example, How do we think about the four empires in our time? Only when the book is rendered complete do we get a sense of the final implied audience.[5] Even if the community represented in the voice of Daniel 10–12 considered itself the implied audience of the entire book, we can see that the Qumran community considered its own time to be the implied audience. The same is true of Jesus and perhaps also John in his apocalypse. This is what happens in repeated, divinely inspired adaptations.

This then brings us to the third permutation of the question regarding implied audience, which will be the focus of this proposition. I have previously mentioned the proposal that the prophetic oracles were collected by later generations who repackaged the prophecies as relevant to their own times and circumstances (proposition 8), but here I want to consider that idea in a larger methodological discussion. In such cases, though the prophet may not have considered them his implied audience, a future generation has identified itself in that way. Note Peter's comment on the day of Pentecost: "The promise is for you and your children and for all who are far off" (Acts 2:39). This therefore pertains to what we call fulfillment.

The relationship between the prophetic message and its fulfillment will be discussed in propositions 10-12. Here the question I want to address is whether the prophets, by virtue of their divine endowment, actually anticipated the ways that their fulfillments would take place. That is, was the generation when the fulfillment took place actually (at least in part) the implied audience of the prophet? More bluntly, does Isaiah know that he is talking about Jesus in Isaiah 7 or in Isaiah 53? Are the Jews who experience the destruction of Herod's

---

[5] As with my comments on Isaiah, I am not going to try to sort through this here, as it would drive us far afield from the focus of this book. For more information about these issues in the book of Daniel, see Aubrey E. Buster and John H. Walton, *The Book of Daniel*, New International Commentary on the Old Testament (Grand Rapids, MI: Eerdmans, forthcoming).

temple by the Romans in AD 70 the implied audience for Daniel's abomination of desolation (Dan 9:27; 11:31; 12:11; Mt 24:15)? Is the generation in which the tribulation is to take place the implied audience of Daniel when he refers to the seventieth week?

I would contend that we have no reason to believe that the prophets have insider knowledge about when or how fulfillment might take place: first, because fulfillment can happen more than once, and second, because fulfillment often takes oblique turns. All of this will be discussed in proposition 11.

As I sum up this discussion of implied audience, I can now propose three categories that may prove helpful:

- The *prophet* has an implied audience that is primarily (if not exclusively) made up of his contemporaries to whom *he* has spoken and to whom his message has meaning.

- The *prophetic book* has an implied audience, members of whom are the target of those who have adapted the messages to their own context and therefore gathered together in writing the prophet's oracles. This could potentially be represented in stages of development of a book (when and if such exist) but is primarily represented in the final collection of the book, now a *written* product *interpreted* as pertaining to them. We rarely have sufficient information to determine who the compiler(s) of this written product might be.

- The *message* of a prophet finds a receptive audience in those who discern that that message has been *fulfilled* in their time. This could happen several times since prophecies can have multiple fulfillments. Unlike the second category, this scenario does not involve accumulating oracles or finalizing or canonizing the book. The book has already achieved that form and status but continues to unfold in people (particularly Jesus) or events that offer connecting dots to the prophets' messages and books.

In traditional perspectives, these three categories are often considered distinctions without differences. Instead, the assumption is that since the prophets operate under divine inspiration, all these layers are considered part of God's intention and God's implied audience. While it may be granted that such a divine perspective is unarguable, when we focus more specifically on the human level, it is difficult to substantiate such a wide-ranging view. A narrower view, perhaps more minimalistic, would see some advantage to recognizing that, rather than the *prophet* having multiple implied audiences, present as well as future, it is *audiences* who adopt for themselves the status of implied audience, whether under the guise of adaptation, accumulation, or fulfillment.[6]

This means that when we seek to interpret the prophets, we would do best to distinguish these varying levels.[7] We first explore the meaning of the prophetic oracles in their own time as best we can (text in context). If the interpreter concludes that there have been stages of accumulation (such as some believe about layers of Isaiah or Daniel), the significance of each layer should be analyzed. The next step is to consider what we know of the final compilation of the book (sadly, often very little) to consider whether those who have committed the collected oracles to writing have adapted its message in some way to their time. Finally, we can consider how the book or the messages it comprises has been interpreted as having been fulfilled by various interpreters in their times. We cannot overstate how much God would have known, but that is not our interpretive question. We could potentially overstate what the prophet knows about his implied audience, so caution would lead us to approach that question minimalistically. Any mistakes that we might make by underestimating the prophet's knowledge would pale in comparison to those mistakes we might make if we overestimate it.

---

[6] I recognize that at times these overlap, that is, that the audience members see fulfillment as taking place in them or in their time.

[7] Note that the same levels are evident in the Gospels.

PART 4

METHODOLOGICAL AND INTERPRETIVE ISSUES

Proposition 10

Distinction Between Message and Fulfillment Provides Clear Understanding of Prophetic Literature

In this proposition I will deal with what may be the most important factor of the methodology essential to a full appreciation of prophetic literature. It is one that I have been alluding to throughout the book. The principle is that if we are to recognize fully the authority of the prophetic books as Scripture, we must give equal and individual attention to two distinct aspects: message and fulfillment.

The *message* is defined as that word from God the prophet intended to deliver to his immediate audience. As I have previously noted, this generally falls into one of four major categories: indictment, judgment, instruction, and aftermath (see proposition 7). The message is one that the prophet understands and one that he expects his audience to understand, even if they fail to respond appropriately to it. The message carries the authority of God, and it does not change over the years, generations, or eras. These messages can be deciphered exegetically using the linguistic, literary, historical, and cultural evidence that is routinely available to interpreters. They are not mystical or encoded; they are not secret or obtuse. Whether general or specific, the prophets delivered their messages in hope of response from their audience, which indicates that the message was discernible.

In contrast, the *fulfillment* is defined as the unfolding of events that brings additional meaning to the original prophetic message. It consists of an event, not a text, and events are not authoritative. Fulfillments, however, are sometimes identified in texts (oral or written), and those identifications can be classified as authoritative depending on whether the one who offers the identification is considered an authoritative instrument of God's revelation. To be more precise, if a New Testament author identifies a fulfillment, we consider that identification to be authoritative by virtue of the authority accorded to that author by God. In contrast, fulfillments identified by you or me, by our pastors, by great Christian theologians of the past, or by cult leaders in a communal compound carry no authority. Though we may observe or experience events that strike us as fulfillments of prophecy, that they are so cannot be validated by exegetical analysis of the prophet's message. The prophets offered no such information. For example, the healing ministry of Jesus could stand as empirical evidence that he is fulfilling prophecy about the Messiah being a healer. However, there were other healers who were not the Messiah. Furthermore, exegetical analysis of the pertinent Old Testament prophecies will not lead to evidence that the prophet had information that his oracle would find fulfillment specifically in Jesus. That is a more subjective assessment, though empirical data about Jesus can be used to substantiate the conclusion.

The prophets expected their prophetic oracles to be fulfilled, but they did not have revelation concerning what that fulfillment might look like. Since they were delivering a word from God, the possibilities were manifold and could take unexpected turns. Regardless of how or when their oracles would be fulfilled, their message had, and continues to have, authority as the word of God.

Message and fulfillment must therefore be distinguished from one another. The message is not altered when the fulfillment takes an

oblique path. Some have been convinced that if the message and fulfillment do not speak in unison, the unity of Scripture is compromised.
I would contend, instead, that they speak in harmony and that there
is no inherent contradiction in doing so. It might be otherwise if, when
the New Testament authors wrote about fulfillment, they were seeking
to identify the message of the prophets. But they were not doing so.
The New Testament writers were not trying to understand the context
of the oracles; they were adapting and repackaging them to new contexts. That is what fulfillment entails. Some examples can help illustrate the principles just laid out.

The classic example is found in the relationship between Hosea 11:1
and Matthew 2:15. In Hosea 11, Yahweh is portrayed as speaking in the
first person. He is reflecting on the history of Israel as he says, "When
Israel was a child, I loved him, / and out of Egypt I called my son." That
historical comment leads into an indictment oracle that contrasts
God's loving treatment of his people and their concomitant faithlessness. The clarity of the message in Hosea 11:1 is indisputable. It is
not the kind of statement that anyone would have read as indicating
future events. Moreover, no one would have thought that it would
have anything to do with the Messiah. When the Jews before the time
of Christ would have compiled lists of prophecies to formulate a messianic profile, this verse would not have been among them. No one
would have insisted that the Messiah would have to come out of Egypt.
It is not a statement that evoked any anticipation of fulfillment.

Despite all of that, Matthew 2:15 unapologetically offers an identification of fulfillment when God instructs Joseph to take his family to
Egypt to escape Herod's jealous rage. Matthew reports that they went
to Egypt and stayed there until Herod died: "And so was fulfilled what
the Lord had said through the prophet, 'Out of Egypt I called my son.'"
Based on my contention that message (what Hosea was talking about)
and fulfillment (the unfolding events in this case surrounding Jesus)
are distinct, we need not accuse Matthew of careless reading or

spurious interpretation. He is not interpreting. Nor do we have to adopt a position that Matthew overrides what seemed transparent in Hosea and try to convince ourselves that Hosea was referring to Jesus all along. Matthew's identified fulfillment does not have to replace Hosea's obvious message. Since Matthew is adapting, not interpreting, the two do not have to be merged into one. At the same time, they could be understood to converge as Matthew develops the unfolding plans and purposes of God. The force of the fulfillment is found not in the idea that Hosea was talking about Jesus but in the idea that Matthew sees Jesus as recapitulating the history of Israel: Israel came out of Egypt, and so did Jesus. Jesus is the new Israel, the better Israel, the true Israel. He reenacts the history of Israel but does not fall prey to faithlessness. He did not have to come out of Egypt to fulfill Hosea 11, but Matthew makes productive use of that event.

With this sort of analysis, we learn that, since Matthew is not *interpreting* Hosea, he is not subject to the kind of hermeneutical controls that we insist on when we are interpreting.[1] Notice that when Peter identifies Jesus as the Messiah (Mt 16:16), Jesus does not praise him for his hermeneutical insight. He does not tell Peter that careful hermeneutical methodology has led him to that conclusion. Instead, Jesus says that it was not by flesh and blood that Peter drew these conclusions "but by my Father in heaven" (Mt 16:17). Peter's insight was the work of inspiration.

Undoubtedly there were principles that guided the *reuse* that was carried out by New Testament authors, but they did not depend on the sort of evidence that we would use. Alternatively, patterns or wordplays would be sufficient.[2] Likewise, we need not conclude that for Matthew to be validated, Hosea must have been talking about Jesus. If

---

[1]For fuller development, see John H. Walton, *Wisdom for Faithful Reading* (Downers Grove, IL: IVP Academic, 2023), 175-79.

[2]For exploration of these, see Richard N. Longenecker, *Biblical Exegesis in the Apostolic Period* (Grand Rapids, MI: Eerdmans, 1975).

we write Matthew's fulfillment over Hosea, we lose the authoritative message of Hosea. If we now go back to Hosea and insist that he be talking about Jesus, we nullify every principle we have that would be used to interpret Hosea.

Fortunately, once we make the essential distinction between message and fulfillment, no such gymnastics are necessary. We can recognize the authoritative message of Hosea as providing a foundation for Matthew's adaptation without feeling the need to make the two identical. Each carries its own authority since message and fulfillment derive their authority through different routes. That is, we recognize Hosea's message as authoritative because we accept that God gave him the oracles that he pronounced. In contrast, we recognize Matthew's identification of fulfillment as authoritative because we accept that it represents insight God gave him as he tracks how the Old Testament was leading toward Jesus in ways that could never have been anticipated by the prophets. In this way, the fact that fulfillment took place in Jesus does not require that the prophets were speaking of Jesus, or even of the Messiah (though sometimes they were). In some cases, the prophets were not speaking *of him*, but what they said nevertheless led *to him*, often in unexpected ways. Once events unfolded, they needed to be identified as fulfillment by sources considered to carry authority.

We can glean further insight and nuance from a second example that compares Isaiah's song of the suffering servant (Is 52:13–53:12) with the numerous New Testament passages that refer back to it.[3] Surprisingly, the New Testament nowhere cites Isaiah 53:6, which would seem to have been the most obvious point of fulfillment. Nevertheless, we learn that Jesus fulfills many of the statements found in this section of Isaiah. Consequently, we can affirm with confidence

---

[3]Mt 8:17; Lk 22:37; Jn 12:38; Acts 8:32-33; Rom 10:16; 15:21; 1 Pet 2:22. Only the Matthew and John citations explicitly indicate a fulfillment, though other passages imply it.

that Jesus is the suffering servant—when we are discussing fulfillment. But what about Isaiah's message?

One must first ask whether Isaiah and his contemporary audience would have considered the servant to be a messianic reference. While Isaiah's portrayal of the servant was certainly a counterintuitive portrait of a king, when the functions of the servant (derived from the four servant songs in Isaiah; see Is 42:1-4; 49:1-6; 50:4-11; 52:13–53:12[4]) are compared to functions of the Messiah (derived from explicit references to messiah in other parts of Isaiah), we find that there is sufficient overlap to see the two profiles as parallel.

That may be well and good at the larger level. However, remembering that the New Testament never refers back to Isaiah 53:6 being fulfilled in Jesus, do we have reason to think that when Isaiah wrote this servant song, he was describing Jesus on the cross? That is, is that inherent in Isaiah's *message*? If not, then what would Isaiah's audience have understood about the message?

I have developed elsewhere the idea that Isaiah is tapping into an Assyrian practice well known at his time, the ritual of the substitute king.[5] In brief, this ritual is used when an omen (usually a lunar eclipse) has been interpreted as suggesting that the king's life is in danger—the gods intend to punish him for some undetermined offense. In an attempt to avert the portended disaster, the king divests himself of his crown and robes, symbolically abdicates the throne, and goes into hiding. A substitute is chosen to take his place—generally someone from the dregs of society. The substitute is given a queen consort and for up to three months performs the ritual duties of the king (though he is not involved in making any real policy decisions). If after that amount of time the substitute does not die, he and his queen are put to death. They are given a royal burial, after which it is

---

[4]Perhaps five if Is 61:1-3 is included.
[5]John H. Walton, "The Imagery of the Substitute King Ritual in Isaiah's Fourth Servant Song," *Journal of Biblical Literature* 122 (2003): 734-43.

determined that the anger of the gods has been appeased. As the texts indicate, he has died for the sins of the people, for which the king is held responsible. Furthermore, we find that these events are, on one occasion, supported by prophetic oracles.[6]

If Isaiah is using this familiar imagery for the suffering servant, his intentions are recognizable even as they are counterintuitive. In his imagery, though the servant is despised, he actually provides a picture of what the true king should be like—giving up his life for the offense of the people. This king is a better one than the king who goes into hiding. Isaiah is therefore giving a new image of what ideal kingship should be—a servant sacrificing for his people. This would have been a radically new idea to the audience of Isaiah, yet an understandable and meaningful one.

The New Testament unsurprisingly finds fulfillment of this picture of a servant king in Jesus. It does not indicate that Jesus' substitutionary atonement is a fulfillment of Isaiah 53 (though later interpreters in church history did not hesitate to connect those dots). Our interpretation of the *message* of Isaiah 53 should not be influenced by those aspects of *fulfillment* that are cited in the New Testament, for the same reason indicated in the last example. Isaiah's message carried authority all on its own in association with what Isaiah's literary intentions were. Those intentions cannot be derived from the fulfillments that are indicated by later authors. By identifying fulfillment, they are not suggesting that Isaiah's message foretold Jesus. Seeing the message and the fulfillment as existing on a continuum allows both to retain their inherent authority. If we reject the New Testament reuse as hermeneutically deficient, or transpose the Old Testament message to a New Testament key, we are undermining the authority of one part of

---

[6]Simo Parpola, *Letters from Assyrian and Babylonian Scholars*, State Archives of Assyria 10 (Helsinki: Helsinki University Press, 1993), text 352; discussion in Martti Nissinen, *References to Prophecy in Neo-Assyrian Sources*, State Archives of Assyria 7 (Helsinki: Neo-Assyrian Text Corpus Project, 1998), 68-77.

Scripture or another. It is not a matching footprint that connects the Testaments; it is a continuum regarding how God's plans and purposes are worked out and coalesce in Jesus, the centerpiece.

For a third example, consider Jesus' quotation of Psalm 22:1 from the cross (Mt 27:46).[7] Even though Matthew does not use the label *fulfillment*, should we think that Psalm 22 is predicting what Jesus will say on the cross? Based on the previous discussion and examples, we can see that there would be no reason to think so. Psalm 22 is a lament psalm and is therefore appropriate for Jesus to allude to as he is dying. The psalmist is not predicting anything about Jesus; Jesus is simply quoting a well-known psalm.

For a final example, I want to turn our attention to Isaiah 7:14, Isaiah's Immanuel prophecy. Matthew 1:23 picks up this prophecy and finds it fulfilled not only in the way that the name Immanuel finds significance in Jesus as God incarnate but in the virgin birth. The question that we must address is to what extent Isaiah 7:14 speaks of the virgin birth of Christ, and the principles that I have suggested for thinking about message and fulfillment will help us to navigate that terrain.

To begin, I note not only that in the NIV the marginal note reads "young woman" but that in every other occurrence of the Hebrew word, NIV translates it that way. Many other translations even translate 'almah' in Isaiah 7:14 as something other than "virgin."[8] So does the word mean "virgin" or not? I have proposed that the Hebrew word 'almah' does not designate a woman who has not yet had a sexual experience (the meaning of the English word *virgin*) but designates a woman who has not yet borne a child.[9] Regardless of how convincing one might find that analysis to be, we can proceed by asking the

---

[7]Note that this is only one of several points of connection that Mt 27 indicates between the crucifixion and Ps 22.

[8]For example, Common English Bible, NET, and NRSV.

[9]John H. Walton, "Isaiah 7:14: What's in a Name?," *Journal of the Evangelical Theological Society* 30, no. 3 (1987): 289-306.

important question, What if '*almah* does not mean "virgin"? Would that negate the virgin birth of Christ? Absolutely not!

According to the relationship that I have proposed between message and fulfillment, there is no need for the fulfillment to be viewed as dictating the meaning of the message. Even beyond the question of the meaning of the word '*almah*, other factors in Isaiah 7 pose insurmountable problems to the idea that Isaiah is talking about the virgin birth of Jesus. Grammatically, the verse uses an adjective in a verbless clause: the '*almah* [is] pregnant (adjective). If this referred to a virgin birth, we would have to acknowledge that there had been a virgin birth in the eighth century BC. The contemporary focus of Isaiah's message is also evident in that in Isaiah 7:15-16 the child is already born and the "two kings" (whom we can easily identify) are no longer a threat. This is not a child that is eight centuries away.

All these observations pose no problem, however, when we again factor in the understanding that the identification of a fulfillment is not a suggestion that Matthew was interpreting the message of the prophet in his context. Isaiah is not talking to his audience about a virgin many centuries in the future who will give birth to the Son of God. His message concerns a young woman (perhaps in the royal household) who has not yet become a mother but is now pregnant with a son. Even in the short amount of time before this son is born (since she is already pregnant), the threat of the armies to the north will dissipate, leading to her giving the boy a name of hope, found in God's presence with his people. The "sign" that Isaiah offers is not that the woman is miraculously pregnant or that she will have a son. The sign is found in the name the son will be given—one that expresses the new hope that has suddenly been realized. A crisis has been averted. This is a highly significant message to the king, his administration, and the people of Jerusalem of Isaiah's time. It carries the authority of God, and we presume that such a son was born.

We are aware that indeed the imminent threat to Jerusalem turned out to be a hollow one that never materialized. In that way, Isaiah's oracle found fulfillment in his own time. Yet, it was to be fulfilled again in part (for instance, no invading armies) in a way that would have never been imagined in Isaiah's day. The fulfillment in Christ also carries authority—not because it represents what Isaiah was saying but because Matthew was given divine insight into this theological truth unfolding in Mary's child. The significance of the name (which had been the sign) is multiplied exponentially since this child is God incarnate. Moreover, the woman's sexual status (explained in the Gospels, that she had not known a man) also took on remarkable new significance.

In the end, our overwriting the prophets' messages with identifications of fulfillment does not strengthen the view of biblical authority; it jeopardizes it. John Barton sees this clearly as he notes that the idea held in common between the Qumran community and early Christianity, that all prophecy pointed to the age in which it would be fulfilled (whether to Christ or to the end times), tended to "devalue or suppress" any reference to the original settings contemporary with the Old Testament writers.[10] Once the premise had been accepted, even vague connections fed into an inexhaustible chain of examples that reflected confirmation bias.

> The belief that Christ had fulfilled all the Scriptures (and was therefore the only true key to their meaning) in one sense dethroned Scripture, for nothing Scripture contained could have any authority unless it fitted with what was believed about him.[11]

---

[10]John Barton, *Oracles of God: Perceptions of Ancient Prophecy in Israel After the Exile* (New York: Oxford University Press, 1986), 194.

[11]Barton, *Oracles of God*, 195. Though Barton may indeed reflect a dismissiveness of the perspectives of the New Testament authors, I am using his quote only to highlight how Old Testament authority could potentially be undermined by misunderstandings about how the New Testament authors are using the Old Testament.

Barton continues by pointing out that this elevates the interpreter to a position of authority in that, as Longenecker indicates, the true message cannot be determined until the *raz* (mystery) and the *pesher* (interpretation) are brought together.[12] It is acceptable for us to adopt the New Testament interpretations as authoritative, but we dare not attribute such authority, a fresh inspiration, to *any* interpreter who promotes any outlandish connection that comes to mind.

In an earlier proposition (9) I raised the question about the authority of repackaged prophecies. In this proposition I have noted that identifications of fulfillment by authoritative voices can be treated as authoritative. Alongside this, I have contended that if the prophet's message carries the authority of Scripture, his intentions must be respected. Consequently, we have recognized a bifurcated authority located separately but equally in message and fulfillment. But what about the practice of adopting a prophecy with an expectation of fulfillment (in contrast to identification of a fulfillment already manifested)? If the adoption of the prophecy, by definition, seeks to extend the prophet's message beyond what he could possibly have known, how can that recontextualization reflect authority? If it does not reflect authority, then how and why does it carry significance?

This is an important question in that I have noted the idea that the actual formation of the canonical prophets appears to have been motivated by later audiences applying the prophets' messages to their own time (proposition 9). To the extent that such is the case, those audiences are perhaps more interested in their repackaged meaning than in the intent of the prophet within the context of his audience. And, as noted, such repackaging is often at the core of people's identification of fulfillment and continues to be what drives any given generation's interest in the prophetic word. How should we sort this out?

---

[12]Barton, *Oracles of God*, 196; Longenecker, *Biblical Exegesis*, 41.

When an audience adapts a prophecy to its own context, such adaptation implies that the audience is receiving the prophecy as authoritative. It is possible, indeed likely, that the acceptance of the validity of such adaptations led to the eventual recognition of the canonical status of the prophetic book (see proposition 9). That does not mean that any given audience throughout history that engaged in repackaging oracles for its own time was doing so correctly. Validation would only come when fulfillment was identified as such by an authoritative voice (for example, the New Testament writers), not with any random person or group's particular proposals. The practice of adopting and redirecting is indicative that the prophets had authority; it cannot be reliably treated as a guide to what the true fulfillment is.

In summary, let's clarify the distinction that I am drawing between interpretation and adaptation. I am referring to text-in-context exegesis focused on the author's literary intentions as *interpretation*.[13] We have noted that this type of analysis leads to an understanding of the message and is where the authority resides. In contrast, what I am calling *adaptation* (or adoption, redirection, or repackaging) refers to what Christians (and even Jews before them) do, from the earliest Christians writing in the New Testament, through the ages of church history, and continuing into today.

In this step I consciously adopt a view of the significance that the prophecy may have to Jesus or even to the events of our own day. Those who fall into this latter category recognize what could be called a "Christotelic" perspective, meaning that we can view prophecy in terms of how it leads to God's plans and purposes being realized in Christ. This is what the New Testament authors were doing and explains Luke 24:25-27 (Jesus' conversation with the travelers on the road to Emmaus) as well as the fulfillments of prophecy. Authority is

---

[13]Granted, this is admittedly an overly narrow definition of interpretation, but bear with me for the sake of explanation. Here this would include those who have given the prophetic books their final shape.

recognized in New Testament repackaging based on the status that we believe those authors have as those who reveal words from God. Their unique authority validates the connections they draw. This is the thrust of 2 Peter 1:20-21. They were not trying to understand the authoritative intentions of the Old Testament. In that way, the New Testament authors were not interpreting (as I have defined it above); they were repackaging, and they saw Christ as the centerpiece of God's plans and purposes. Old Testament texts invite Christotelic *repackaging*; they do not demand *reinterpretation* of the Old Testament as being about Christ.

In conclusion, all of this should lead us to be extremely cautious about adopting an understanding of the prophets based on fulfillment *we* might identify or anticipate. Prophecy is not all about fulfillment; it is all about the proclamation of God's plans and purposes. When we see fulfillment, we are reminded that God is at work carrying out his plans and purposes even when they take a very different shape from what was expected. We should not think that we can anticipate the shape of fulfillment as we recognize that even the prophets themselves, as well as the New Testament authors, were often surprised by how fulfillment took place, or disappointed that it did not seem to be taking place the way that they expected. These oblique trajectories will be addressed specifically in the next proposition.

Fulfillment Follows
Oblique Trajectories

Anyone who has either compared prophetic messages to identified fulfillments or explored the lack of fulfillment in particular cases will not be surprised to learn that fulfillment follows oblique trajectories. Nowhere is this clearer than in the ways that Jesus fulfills prophecy in unexpected ways or does not fulfill prophecy in ways that would have been anticipated. Most obvious is that Jesus was not a king in any of the expected ways. This should warn us that having the prophetic oracles available to us does not mean that we have clear vision regarding what fulfillment will look like. This is so because, as the evidence indicates, the prophetic oracles do not reliably lead to a straight-line deduction of what fulfillment would look like. Several categories can highlight examples of why a flexible perspective is required.

When people change their course, projected fulfillment can be forestalled or eliminated. As I have previously mentioned, this indicates that, at least at times, prophecy is characterized by conditionality. Since that is the case, fulfillment of any sort (let alone a certain sort) is not assured. In Nineveh's case, their change for the better nullified (or at least postponed) the fulfillment of Jonah's prophecy. In the case

of Eli and his house (1 Sam 2:30) it went the other way: the promise
made to the priestly family was withdrawn.

Fulfillment can occur multiple times. This is evidenced in the abomination of desolation referred to several times in Daniel, which is fulfilled both in the second century BC and in the first century AD. In
addition, Israel's return to the land happens several times in different
ways. Consequently, the acknowledgment that a prophecy has been
fulfilled in one way at one time does not rule out a different sort of
fulfillment at another time.

Fulfillment may be altered. A hallmark example of this is found in
Daniel 9, when Daniel is informed that the restoration expected after
seventy years will now stretch out over nearly five centuries.

Fulfillment may not look like what would have been anticipated. A
very simple example can be found in Judges 4:9, where Deborah indicates that the Lord will deliver the enemy into "the hands of a woman."
Since this comes in the context of Barak insisting that he will not go
unless Deborah goes with him, surely the immediate audience would
have expected that Deborah was speaking about herself. Modern
readers find that also to be the most expected outcome. Who would
have ever thought that it would be fulfilled by the relatively unknown
Jael (Judg 4:22; 5:24-27)?

Isaiah 13:19-22 provides another example:

> Babylon, the jewel of kingdoms,
>   the pride and glory of the Babylonians,
> will be overthrown by God
>   like Sodom and Gomorrah.
> She will never be inhabited
>   or lived in through all generations;
> there no nomads will pitch their tents,
>   there no shepherds will rest their flocks.
> But desert creatures will lie there,
>   jackals will fill her houses;

there the owls will dwell,
>   and there the wild goats will leap about.
Hyenas will inhabit her strongholds,
>   jackals her luxurious palaces.
Her time is at hand,
>   and her days will not be prolonged.

The elaborate details of this passage would give any reader a level of confidence about what the eventual demise of Babylon would look like. To the casual reader, the comparison to Sodom and Gomorrah suggests a sudden, total destruction from fire raining from heaven. Furthermore, the only inhabitants would be chaos creatures with no human occupants in sight. Moreover, one could easily conclude that the fulfillment would happen in the near future for Isaiah's audience. That is how it would make sense to Isaiah's audience.

In contrast, the testimony of history and archaeology give a very different picture. It is clear that Babylon remained dominant even after being conquered by Cyrus in 539 BC. This high status is still evident throughout the two centuries of Persian rule.[1] In the Hellenistic period, Babylon continued to have importance for Alexander and remained a major center of the Seleucids, already six centuries removed from the time of Isaiah. Babylon eventually slipped into insignificance, not having been destroyed by conquerors, let alone by fire falling from heaven. Instead, apparently the shifting course of the Euphrates was responsible for relegating it to irrelevance and obscurity as it was gradually abandoned. In that way, it did become the ruin inhabited by chaos creatures to which Isaiah refers. The problem here is not unfulfilled prophecy but the way that particular

---

[1]Herodotus reports the revolt of Babylon against Xerxes that took place in 479 BC and, further, that there was some destruction in Babylon at that time. There are nevertheless questions about Herodotus's report, and, even if it is true, Babylon remained largely intact and an important city. Pierre Briant, *From Cyrus to Alexander: A History of the Persian Empire* (Winona Lake, IN: Eisenbrauns, 2002), 544-45.

details (sudden destruction and timing) never worked out in the expected ways.

This apparent disconnect is no problem when we recognize the oblique pathways that fulfillment can take. When we recognize that prophecy is not predicting the future and that fulfillment can follow numerous alternative paths, such texts will no longer stand as problematic. Yet anyone trying to imagine the end times in the time of Isaiah would never have been able to accurately anticipate the details of Babylon's fate.

A final example can be found in Isaiah 11:15-16, where, speaking of Ephraim and Judah, the prophet says:

> The LORD will dry up
>   the gulf of the Egyptian sea;
> with a scorching wind he will sweep his hand
>   over the Euphrates River.
> He will break it up into seven streams
>   so that anyone can cross over in sandals.
> There will be a highway for the remnant of his people
>   that is left from Assyria,
> as there was for Israel
>   when they came up from Egypt.

Ephraim refers to the northern kingdom of Israel, which in the time of Isaiah was defeated by the Assyrians and carried into exile. Here the prophet speaks of a return in striking terms. A Red Sea–type experience like that witnessed by the Israelites coming out of Egypt centuries earlier is seen as God's mechanism for delivering the people of the Northern Kingdom and returning them en masse from their exile.

As we examine the records of history (whether in the Bible or elsewhere), we find nothing that would approach this sort of outcome for the Northern Kingdom exiles. Every indication is that they were assimilated into the peoples among whom the Assyrians had scattered them.

Nothing suggests that they ever returned at all, let alone in the way that Isaiah suggests. Furthermore, it would be challenging to maintain that it may still happen since there is no remaining trace of the Northern Kingdom (aside from those who remained in the land and eventually joined the people of Judah).

This example is perhaps the most problematic of all among those we have considered because not only does there seem to be no fulfillment at all, but there is apparently no longer any chance of fulfillment. Similar examples can be found in Isaiah 17:1, which says that Damascus will no longer be a city (though it continues to exist even until today), and Ezekiel 30:10-11, which says that Nebuchadnezzar will destroy Egypt, something that is difficult to substantiate historically.[2] Regardless of whether historical validation can be suggested or not, examples such as these should not cause us to doubt the credibility of prophecy. Rather, they should prompt us to reevaluate how we think about prophecy and fulfillment.

If fulfillment can take oblique turns from the message, be altered, or at times seem never to have happened at all, we need to return to Deuteronomy 18:22: "If what a prophet proclaims in the name of the LORD does not take place or come true, that is a message the LORD has not spoken. That prophet has spoken presumptuously, so do not be alarmed."[3] I agree with the important caveats that Eric Tully raises.[4] He notes first that this criterion can only pertain to oracles that focus on the near future; otherwise, the audience could not use fulfillment as validation. Second, he recognizes that this criterion obviously could not work if a judgment oracle was conditional. In such a situation the judgment may not come about because the audience responded

---

[2] I am grateful to Jim Walton for providing these examples. He cited these as examples that skeptics bring to discussions as they attempt to discredit the Bible.
[3] Cf. supporting statements in 1 Sam 3:19-20; Jer 28:9; and Ezek 33:33.
[4] Eric J. Tully, *Reading the Prophets as Christian Scripture* (Grand Rapids, MI: Baker Academic, 2022), 80.

positively. In that case, the prophet's status as one speaking the word of God is not compromised.

In the end, the cautions in Deuteronomy 18 and other similar passages are unrelated to the complications with fulfillment that have been addressed above. The scenario in Deuteronomy 18:22 is transparently associated with a short-term judgment oracle since it indicates that the people should not be alarmed (a response to judgment oracles). It does not indicate that they will know a word *is* from God when it does come true. It only affirms the inverse; they will know it is *not* from God when it does *not* come true.[5]

In most of the cases noted above, the fulfillment does come about, but in unexpected ways. In a case such as Isaiah 11, Isaiah's track record has already confirmed him as a true prophet so his authenticity is no longer in question. The very fact that the book of Isaiah is preserved by a later generation and perhaps supplemented over centuries demonstrates that. The oracle in Isaiah 11 is therefore an outlier, and, in light of Isaiah's confirmed status, we should suspend judgment or at least recognize that our expectations of fulfillment were more narrow than necessary.[6]

---

[5]John H. Walton, *Ancient Near Eastern Thought and the Old Testament*, 2nd ed. (Grand Rapids, MI: Baker Academic, 2018), 250.
[6]Moreover, note that it is an aftermath oracle, not a judgment oracle, in which case Deut 18 has less relevance.

The New Testament Use
of Old Testament Prophecy Focuses
on Fulfillment, Not Message

Luke 24, mentioned in passing in the last proposition, is a touchstone for many who are sorting out how Jesus relates to the Old Testament. The issue is wide ranging and not limited to only particular genres. I cannot address the whole scope of the question here but will focus on one aspect of it, namely, the way that Jesus factors into prophecy.[1]

Of particular interest to us are the verses Luke 24:27, 44: "And beginning with Moses and all the Prophets, he explained to them what was said in all the Scriptures concerning himself. . . . Everything must be fulfilled that is written about me in the Law of Moses, the Prophets and the Psalms." Luke 24:27 indicates that the Old Testament has information about Jesus. He does not limit the source material to prophetic literature since he refers to "all Scripture." While this potentially makes *any* Scripture a resource, it does not necessarily imply that *every* Scripture speaks of him. This would therefore likewise mean that *any* prophecy may be fulfilled in him but certainly does not suggest that *every*

---

[1]I have addressed the broader discussion in my book *Wisdom for Faithful Reading* (Downers Grove, IL: IVP Academic, 2023), 70-78.

prophetic oracle finds fulfillment in him. Rather, it indicates that he explained to them how all sorts of Scriptures pertained to him. We can imagine that he would not have had the time to explain every passage of Scripture, so we can infer his coverage was selective and perhaps representative. The sentence qualifies that he showed them the ones that *did* pertain to him, which falls short of saying that all of them pertain to him.

Luke 24:44 speaks specifically about fulfillment, but by including the three categories (Law, Prophets, and Psalms) we can infer that *fulfillment* is a word that is not limited in application to prophetic oracles. As in Luke 24:27, this statement has built-in qualifiers. Everything that can be said to be written about him must be fulfilled. What would that list look like? Again, it does not suggest that everything in the three categories was written about him, but whatever was written about him must be fulfilled. Arguably, Jesus is not here making a hermeneutical statement about prophecy and fulfillment but is indicating that his work must be completed as it is delineated in Scripture.

Since both verses have built-in qualifiers, they leave us uninformed about how extensive the references may have been. More importantly, we would search in vain to find any hermeneutical controls that could guide us in determining which verses speak about Jesus, how we recognize them, and what they say about him. The hermeneutical problem is that since the Old Testament writers themselves, prophets included, show no indication that their message and intention extend to specific details about Jesus, any identification of how those passages (however many or few there are) pertain to Jesus must reach outside the author's intentions to make the connection. If we do not have the author's intentions to guide us with a sure method, what are the controls? Can anyone connect any passage to Jesus in any way? Without controls, we can certainly imagine that abuse could result. If such connections are the result of only the interpreter's imagination, then such connective suggestions are not verifiable and not falsifiable. How then can they be considered meaningful? How could they be considered essential?

This is the black hole of the hermeneutics regarding the New Testament use of the Old Testament.

One way to resolve this dilemma is to take a minimalist approach. In this approach, only the fulfillments that are cited in the New Testament are considered credible. Their credibility is a result of the prior conclusion that those writers have authority. In this situation, authorial intention remains the criterion, even though it is the New Testament author's intention, not that of the Old Testament authors. The strength of this method is that it is characterized by clearly defined controls. Christians have been reluctant to adopt this view because it rules out many Old Testament passages and their proposed fulfillments that have long been held dear by the church.[2]

The concept of biblical authority is guarded by controls applied to interpretation. If the concepts of fulfillment drawn out of Luke 24 do not provide controls, then we cannot use them with any confidence and still maintain a view of biblical authority. Fulfillments can only be validated if they have an authoritative voice behind them.

This minimalistic approach then raises the problem of a double standard. We do not know what controls were used by New Testament authors (or even by Jesus himself), and none are evident to us, so how can we consider their resulting identifications of fulfillment to be valid and to have authority? We might conclude that they used methods that were familiar and accepted in their time (and thus had whatever controls that thinking could afford) and made sense to them, but the first-century methods of which we are aware do not, in general, commend themselves to modern hermeneutics.[3]

---

[2]Included in this are Old Testament passages such as Gen 3:15, widely claimed to be prophetic, as well as the proposed typology of the tabernacle or the Song of Solomon. Cases such as these make up a high percentage of lists of fulfilled prophecies in apologetic books. For one example, see the list from the Josh McDowell Ministry Team, "Did Jesus Fulfill Old Testament Prophecy?," accessed May 3, 2023, www.josh.org/jesus-fulfill-prophecy/.

[3]Discussed in detail in Richard N. Longenecker, *Biblical Exegesis in the Apostolic Period* (Grand Rapids, MI: Eerdmans, 1975). In the same way, the methods of Origen made sense

One obvious resolution is to acknowledge that we recognize their authority based on the inspiration that we have reason to believe was at work in them. People who are inspired do not need a consistent methodology. Inspiration validates when hermeneutics cannot do so. No one after the New Testament can claim inspiration. Consequently, we are not free to do what the New Testament authors do—at least not with the confidence of reliable results.

We should also note that most of what the New Testament authors recognized as fulfilled had already taken place—in most cases surrounding Jesus. Once they recognized Jesus as the Son of God and the promised Messiah, they found ample reason to view him as fitting that job description by means of more obscure connections. They were not, however, offering glimpses of the future (end times) based on potential fulfillments of prophecies. For them, fulfillment focused on Jesus and had the benefit of hindsight.

This means that modern practices of trying to determine the shape of the end times find no precedent in the Evangelists or Paul. Jesus occasionally made some comments, as in the Olivet Discourse, but then it was to emphasize that we could *not* successfully determine the appearance of the end time—the sequence of events or when it would occur.

---

to him and, in his view, had controls (theological in nature), yet we could not employ them today with controls that work in our perspective.

EXCURSUS: MESSIANIC PROPHECY

Since Jesus, the Messiah, fulfilled numerous prophecies that were not evidently viewed as messianic in their Old Testament context, we have to be careful about how we define messianic prophecy. If we defined it based on message, we would look for an indication that the prophet was discussing a future, ideal, Davidic king. As seen in table 12.1, that would narrow the field to just a handful of passages. I propose instead that we should define it based on fulfillment rather than on message. That is to say, a prophecy may be considered more broadly messianic when it is one that, according to the New Testament, finds fulfillment in Jesus, regardless of whether the message of the prophet was messianic.

With this definition, verses that I have already discussed, such as Isaiah 7:14 and Hosea 11:1, may legitimately be classified as messianic prophecies even though in Isaiah and Hosea they would not have been recognized as such by either the prophet or his audience. At the same time, this definition would not include Genesis 3:15 since the message in Genesis does not identify a victor. Blows exchanged on both sides are potentially fatal, but not necessarily so. Furthermore, the New Testament never identifies Jesus as fulfilling it.[a]

If the defining feature of messianic prophecy is that it is recognized either as having a messianic message (by the prophet himself or later in the Old Testament) or as having been fulfilled by Jesus, the list of such prophecies is much more abbreviated than claims found in apologetics books. Table 12.1 delineates five categories to help sort through the various scenarios.

Table 12.1. Classification of messianic prophecy (based on when recognized)

CLASS	WHEN RECOGNIZED	KEY ELEMENTS	EXAMPLES
I	Recognized as messianic by the prophet when spoken (in message)	Ideal, future, Davidic king	Is 9:6-7; 11:1-16; Jer 23:5-6; 30:9; Ezek 37:21-28; Amos 9:11; Mic 5:2-5; Zech 9:9
II	Recognized as messianic by later Old Testament authors (becomes part of expectation)	Cited in later class I context	Gen 49:10 (Ps 60:7; 108:8); 2 Sam 7:12-16 (Ps 89)
III	Recognized as messianic during the intertestamental period	Found in literature such as the Apocrypha, Pseudepigrapha, and Dead Sea Scrolls	Num 24:17-19; Deut 18:18-19
IV	Recognized as messianic by New Testament authors after the fact (in fulfillment)	If these fulfillments had not taken place, Christ's messianic claim would not have been thereby denied.	Ps 22; Is 7:14; Hos 11:1; Zech 12:10
V	Recognized as messianic by the church after the fact with no support from text*	Tradition and consensus important to establish credibility, but lower in level of authority	Gen 3:15

*By the definition that I offered, this category would not be considered messianic prophecy since the New Testament does not validate the fulfillment.

Source: Adapted from John H. Walton and Andrew E. Hill, *Old Testament Today*, 2nd ed. (Grand Rapids, MI: Zondervan, 2013), 284.

It is worth noting that even those in class I of the table, though clearly messianic in the prophet's understanding, do not always connect seamlessly to fulfillment. A brief summary of each will make the point.

- Isaiah 9:6-7 clearly talks about a future, ideal, Davidic king, thus having a messianic message. Even though this is Jesus' destiny (Lk 1:33), it is not fulfilled by Jesus in the New Testament. Even though I readily accept an already/not yet perspective, he does not sit on David's throne in the New Testament, where fulfillment would have been expected to take certain forms (as evident in the reactions of all parties during Jesus' earthly ministry), regardless of how adjustments have been made throughout church history.

- Isaiah 11:1-16 contains almost nothing fulfilled by Jesus during his lifetime. One possible exception is the idea that the Spirit will rest on him (Is 11:2; cf. Jn 1:32-33).

- Jeremiah 23:5-6; 30:9 is fulfilled in Jesus as one from the line of David, but that is simply the definition of *messiah*. Again, he does not actually sit on David's throne. These verses are not cited in the New Testament as fulfilled by Jesus.

- Ezekiel 37:21-28 talks about the kingship of the Messiah uniting the tribes of Israel, establishing an enduring covenant with them, and says that all the nations will recognize him. None of this is cited as fulfilled in the New Testament or actually took place while Jesus was on earth.

- Amos 9:11 speaks of the renewal of David's kingdom—again neither cited in the New Testament nor yet fulfilled by Jesus in any recognizable sense. It is quoted in Acts 15:16-17, but in reference to the inclusion of the Gentiles, not in reference to the messianic role of Jesus.

- Micah 5:2-5 was already discussed above in proposition 3. This is cited in the New Testament and fulfilled by Jesus with regard to the detail (born in Bethlehem) but not distinctly in the larger, more important issue of being a new start to the Davidic line.

- Zechariah 9:9 is cited as fulfilled in Matthew 21:5, but again the fulfillment rests on an inconsequential detail—riding a donkey. The thrust of the prophecy in Zechariah was that he was coming as a king. Riding on a donkey was just what kings would do. The triumphal entry is also related to kingship to the extent that Christ was offering himself as king. Nevertheless, he is not accepted as king, so that part of the prophecy, the most important part, was neither cited as fulfilled nor actually accomplished.

One passage that, because of some ambiguity, is not on the chart will provide additional data.

Isaiah 61:1-2 is read by Jesus in the synagogue along with his indication that he is the fulfillment of it (Lk 4:18-19). In the context of Isaiah, the speaker can be compared favorably to the servant figure earlier in the book. To the extent that the servant can be identified as a messianic figure (note the use of "anointed" in Is 61:1), I would then conclude that this passage could be categorized as a class I prophecy. Others claim that the speaker is the prophet himself, who proclaims what the Lord is doing (not what is being done through or by him).

Nevertheless, as has often been noted by those dealing with the intersection of Isaiah and Luke here, it is less certain whether Jesus is including the whole section of Isaiah 61 as that which he is now fulfilling or just the verses that he reads. The point I would like to make is that even here, the nature and extent of fulfillment is complex. These examples illustrate that class I prophecies, even though they are clearly identifiable as messianic with regard to the prophet's message, generally are not cited in the New Testament as finding their main point of fulfillment in the life of Jesus. Instead, Christians look forward to fulfillment of these aspects of prophecy in the second coming of Christ. Even as citation and fulfillment of class I prophecies are largely absent from the New Testament, class IV prophecies, those most often cited as fulfilled in Christ by New Testament authors, are precisely those that did not have any identifiable messianic intent in the original prophecies. That is, as noted in the chart, class IV passages would not have defined messianic expectation at the time of Christ, and, if they had not been accomplished in him, they could not have been used to refute messianic claims made by him or on his behalf.

The essential messianic prophecies (class I) were largely not fulfilled, while the nonessential ones (class IV) are cited as fulfilled.[b] What should we make of this? Since class I prophecies are defined by the elements of ideal, future, Davidic kingship, and since Jesus did not actually assume the throne of David or take up an earthly kingship, it is no surprise that no class I prophecies are cited as fulfilled by New Testament authors, except in incidentals. In contrast, since class IV prophecies are defined as not having a messianic message in their Old Testament contexts, they can only be identified as messianic if the definition pertains to fulfillment. In point of fact, then, the New Testament citations of fulfillment focus almost exclusively on passages that did not have a messianic *message* in their original context.

At this point we must consider the citation of psalms in the New Testament as being fulfilled.[c] The first question to address is, in which class should these be categorized? One of the major complications concerns whether the enthronement psalms are focused on a king from the psalmist's day or on a future, ideal, Davidic king. On the one hand, there are indisputably idealistic features that were never fulfilled by the kings of Judah. But, on the other hand, we would not be surprised if enthronement celebrations were aspirational as the Israelites hoped for the best from the newly crowned king. Even though the psalms are ostensibly in a different genre from the classical prophets, some of them are presented as oracles. This leads John Hilber to classify some of them as "cultic prophecy"[d]— a subcategory of prophetic literature as much as a subcategory of psalms. Even those that are not presented as oracles may yet qualify for being fulfilled in the same way that Hosea

11:1, an oracle referring to the past, could become the subject of fulfillment. Any word of God could plausibly be subject to fulfillment regardless of whether it is oracular or visionary, on one hand, or narrative or hymnic, on the other.

To return to the question of how they would be classified on the chart, I would not put psalms such as Psalm 2 or Psalm 110 into class I if they are speaking of the ideal nature of the present king rather than speaking more abstractly about an ideal future king. Those would be in class II. Other psalms, such as Psalm 16, have no explicit royal aspect to them—they simply speak of a faithful person. No Israelite would have read Psalm 16 as prophesying anything about the Messiah. Consequently, this belongs in class IV.

---

[a]For further discussion of this issue, including extensive treatment of Rom 16:20, see John H. Walton and J. Harvey Walton, *Demons and Spirits in Biblical Theology* (Eugene, OR: Cascade Books, 2019), 141-43. To make a specific point, it is not clear that Paul is even referring to Rom 16:20 because the verb he uses is not the one used in the Septuagint of Gen 3:15, and, more importantly, he speaks of Satan under the foot rather than under the heel. Putting enemies under one's foot is a well-known image in the ancient world.

[b]Note that class II and class III prophecies are generally not cited in the New Testament, even though they are picked up in early Christian interpretation as being messianic.

[c]One author's extensive list includes Ps 2; 8; 12; 16; 20–22; 40–41; 45; 68–69; 72; 93; 101–102; 109–110; 118; 129. See Gerard van Groningen, *Messianic Revelation in the Old Testament* (Grand Rapids, MI: Baker Books, 1990), 333-404.

[d]For detailed discussion of this possibility, see John W. Hilber, *Cultic Prophecy in the Psalms* (Berlin: De Gruyter, 2005).

In conclusion, in this proposition I have suggested that, based on a careful distinction between message and fulfillment, we can see that the New Testament shows much more interest in revealing fulfillment than in a text-in-context interpretation of the Old Testament prophets. This does not subordinate the fulfillment, nor does it undervalue the contributions of the New Testament. I only suggest that we need to recognize the different tasks that they have. This in turn can caution us about pronouncing how prophecies have been or might be fulfilled when we have no New Testament precedent for such identifications of fulfillment.

Prophecy Carries Important Implications for Understanding God and the Future, but Our Ability to Forge a Detailed Eschatology with Confidence Is Limited

What does the Olivet Discourse (particularly Mt 24:30-35) tell us about God and the future? These words of Jesus give us little basis on which to build a definitive timeline of the future; in fact, Jesus himself denies that it can be done. The verses are about the ongoing role of Jesus in the eventual establishment of the kingdom of God (which is also what the prophets that Jesus is referring to were talking about), not about eschatological schemes.[1] Jesus remains central. The future plans and purposes of God remain focused on the role of Jesus—until the end of time, whatever that turns out to look like or whenever it occurs. It is not just that Jesus wins (an arguably reductionistic summary of the message of the book of Revelation), but Jesus is the centerpiece. He not only became incarnate at a critical juncture to provide salvation; he is the one through

---

[1]For more detailed discussion of the Olivet Discourse, see proposition 16.

whom the redemption of all creation is to take place, resulting in the new heaven and new earth.[2]

This is in line with what prophecy in general tells us about the future. In the Old Testament, it is not so much the idea that God has fully determined the future and knows and controls its every detail, though some might go that direction at least in part. Alternatively, the point is that though history may unfold in a variety of ways, its eventual outcome has been determined by God and cannot be thwarted.[3] There may be all sorts of detours and roadblocks along the way, thus undermining our attempts to plot a sure course, but the result is assured—the kingdom of God will come.

The future is in God's hands, but the details of the future have not been made known to us. Our hope and faith are therefore focused on God, and our expectations fix their gaze on the establishment of the kingdom of God in Christ. The prophets spoke of Israel's future in the covenant, Matthew spoke of Jesus' future, and apocalyptic (Daniel and Revelation) spoke of the kingdom's future. None of this provides a foundation for a detailed eschatology—a proposition to which I now turn our attention.

John Barton suggests two different ways of thinking about eschatology.[4] The first features a belief that God has a grand plan that will eventually reach its culmination as he determines its proper time. The second looks the same with the exception that it features the belief that the culmination is upon us and that we are living in the last days of that grand plan. This latter group is "reading the signs" and identifying what they believe to be the fulfillment of prophecies.

---

[2]Suggesting this focus is not intended to imply that no details given by Jesus are of ongoing importance. Rather, it limits what role this passage plays in developing eschatological systems.

[3]This should be understood not as a view of history claimed by open theists but rather as an attempt to avoid too meticulous a view of providence.

[4]John Barton, *Oracles of God: Perceptions of Ancient Prophecy in Israel After the Exile* (New York: Oxford University Press, 1986), 218. By calling them "different" I am not suggesting that they are mutually exclusive. Some interpreters succeed in holding them in tension.

The latter differs from the former in the conviction that the end is imminent, not necessarily true of the first. I have proposed that when we read the prophets according to text in context, the grand plan of God is seen in the context of the covenant with Israel, and its culmination will reflect the realization of the covenant blessings. Apocalyptic literature, which will be treated separately below (proposition 14), opens the door to a more universal perspective beyond Israel and her covenant.[5]

In either of Barton's two ways of thinking, readers may be inclined to develop intricate timelines for how the final era of humankind's history will unfold. This elicits the question that I have been leading up to throughout this book and will now address explicitly: *Do we have the textual wherewithal to identify such timelines and incorporate specific events into them?*

We can now address the issue of eschatology beyond systems. To do so we can contrast the ideal covenant hope of the Israelites to the transcendent hope that developed as the New Testament and the church adopted those Old Testament passages and enhanced them based on the teaching and acts of Jesus.

One aspect of Israel's covenant hope was that Yahweh would bring deliverance from the nation's enemies. The corresponding, yet contrasting transcendent hope of the church is that God, through Christ, has saved his people from their sins. Continuity is found in that both feature deliverance; discontinuity is found in what they are being delivered from and what they are being delivered to. The people of Israel are delivered to an existence of rest in their covenant land. The church is delivered to the kingdom rest that Jesus offers (Mt 11:28) and that will be finally fulfilled at a future time (Heb 4). Continuity is found in both being forms of kingdom rest.

---

[5]To be sure, the classical prophets are not devoid of such perspectives, but in apocalyptic they take center stage.

EXCURSUS: ESCHATOLOGICAL SYSTEMS
AND THEIR LIMITATIONS

I was raised in the context of dispensational-ism with its characteristic features of a premillennial, pretribulation rapture just prior to a great tribulation lasting seven years. In this view, the church age was a parenthesis in God's plan. The position is supported primarily with apocalyptic texts such as Daniel and Revelation, supplemented by passages such as the Olivet Discourse (Mt 24) and 1 Thessalonians 4. In this view, at the right time, accompanied by signs (such as the building of the third temple and the appearance of the antichrist), Jesus would return and take (rapture) his people, the church, an event that would inaugurate the seventieth week of Daniel, the seven years of the great tribulation. This would then be followed by the millennial reign of Christ, the war of Armageddon, and the final judgment.

This is the perspective that is represented in some highly popularized eschatological works such as Hal Lindsey's *The Late Great Planet Earth* and the twelve-volume fictional re-creation known as the Left Behind series by Tim LaHaye and Jerry Jenkins. Of course, other competing eschatological systems, such as amillennialism, posttribulationism, postmillennialism, and historical premillen-nialism, exist as alternatives, even if never enjoying the wild popularity of the aforementioned books.

For many readers these may be meaningless technical systems of which they have little understanding and even less interest in. But for other readers this world of competing eschatological systems has dominated their churches or institutions, framed their interaction with the prophets, and may even stand at the core of their theology. Even readers who are mystified by the details of the various eschatological systems have often adopted the expectation of the rapture and great tribulation as essential elements of their theology.

I am not going to spend time presenting these systems in detail or critiquing the particular presuppositions that lead people to espouse one over the other.[a] We might well ask, however, whether eschatology deserves as prominent a place in theology as some give it, or whether a systematic treatment of eschatology is even possible. So instead of considering one system over another, I want to consider very briefly the question of the premise of systematic eschatology.

The study of eschatology in systematic theology represents an attempt to accumulate what we can know and believe about the end times. As with all areas of systematics, it seeks to be based on Scripture (using both Testaments[b]) but also relies to some extent on philosophy and logic for its conclusions. The challenge of systematics is to do its job without falling prey to imposing foreign (modern) ideas onto these important ancient texts. Donald Gowan expresses this well when he observes that the original teachings of the Bible, when interpreted and used to construct theology, "have been mingled with a great variety of philosophies over the centuries and frequently have been distorted to the point where their new forms are scarcely compatible with their sources."[c] I believe that the church can renew a more biblical focus with what is called "holistic eschatology," which focuses attention on the redemption of all creation.[d]

This is important both from a theological standpoint and from a methodological one. Theologically, heeding the warnings of scholars such as Richard Middleton and N. T. Wright will help us to focus beyond ourselves ("I am saved and going to heaven"), recognizing instead that God's plans and purposes pertain to all of creation. Methodologically, the perspective that this book has been promoting suggests that apocalyptic literature is not conducive to the formulation of systems that try to work out all the details. I would contend that it is simply not doing what those who formulate such systems believe that it is doing.

My position today does not adopt any of the eschatological systems. As is evident, I believe that any systemization in this theological field risks overreach. Just as the Bible is not meant to provide a guide to finding God's will for decision-making as we go through life, a comprehensive moral system, a history of the world, a systematic theology, or an answer to all of our social questions,[e] it is likewise not meant to provide a template for eschatology. The Bible is less interested in future events than in the fact of the future kingdom of God. In this I follow Middleton's observation that eschatology is not primarily about our personal salvation or about end-time events. Instead, he emphasizes a "holistic vision of God's intent to renew or redeem creation"— which he refers to as "the Bible's best-kept secret."[f] In contrast to popular perception, the shape of the end times is beyond our reach and above our paygrade. Eschatology therefore provides us with a current objective—to live as God's people in a troubled world. It also provides us with an impetus to do so—the hope that we have in God's kingdom and Christ's eternal reign.[g] The focus of our eschatology is therefore easy enough: God's kingdom will come, and it will feature Jesus, the risen Savior and the reigning King— Immanuel and Messiah. Eschatology therefore should reflect the expectation that Christ will return to establish an eternal kingdom on earth that will be characterized by the

redemption of all creation in a fully ordered state of harmonious relationship. It has no need for timelines or interpretation of symbols, and it is not about us going to heaven but about heaven coming to earth.

Rejecting the idea of a system is not the same as rejecting hope. We do not have to schedule hope or chart out its parameters. We need to clutch it to our hearts and cherish it as the comfort God gives in troubled times. We trust the details to God.

---

[a]Others have done this work. For example, see J. Richard Middleton, *A New Heaven and a New Earth: Reclaiming Biblical Eschatology* (Grand Rapids, MI: Baker Academic, 2014), 221-27, 300-303, for a detailed discussion of passages that putatively refer to the rapture.

[b]Describing an Old Testament eschatology would be part of the effort of biblical theology rather than a reflection of systematics. For an example of this approach, see Donald E. Gowan, *Eschatology in the Old Testament* (Minneapolis: Fortress, 1986). The approach in systematics offers inherent challenges since Old Testament eschatology could not possibly have included the most important tenets of our current systematic eschatology.

[c]Gowan, *Eschatology*, 121.

[d]Middleton, *New Heaven and a New Earth*, 303-12, offers what I have found to be the most helpful discussion of this view. He cites support from the neo-Calvinist movements launched by Kuyper and Bavinck as well as found in Wesleyan traditions. He likewise garners lists of those popular writers who follow a similar path, from Tim Keller to N. T. Wright.

[e]For discussion of all of these, see John H. Walton, *Wisdom for Faithful Reading* (Downers Grove, IL: IVP Academic, 2023). Note that I am not claiming the Bible is lacking wisdom for decision-making, moral perspectives, history, theology, or wisdom for pondering social issues. I contend, instead, that all of these are tangential to the Bible's main purpose.

[f]Middleton, *New Heaven and a New Earth*, 24.

[g]Gowan provides a similar focus on object and impetus, *Eschatology*, 125.

Building on that idea, a second comparison is between Israel's covenant hope—focused on the restoration of the covenant community as a future ideal kingdom of God—and the church's hope, which focuses on the eventual restoration of full order that transcends history to bring the eternal kingdom of God in the new heaven and new earth. Third, the respective ideas of kingdom are characterized by the understanding of the king. Israel looks to the reign of an ideal Davidic king to maintain covenant faithfulness and covenant blessings. The church finds that Davidic king in Jesus, the king who, though having taken on humanity, transcends humanity as the Son of God.

It is the covenant hope of Israel that is addressed in both prophetic and apocalyptic literatures. The transcendent hope of the church is derived from them more than it is addressed in them. These features all reflect the corresponding ideas, but, as mentioned above, important contrasts also affect ideas of kingdom, salvation, kingship, and eschatology. The ideals of the Israelite hope were temporal; they were adopted into Christianity as atemporal, transcending their original context. Such a shift is not illegitimate, nor should it be neglected. But we must realize that the ideal covenant hopes of Israel do not anticipate or speak to the transcendent hope that develops in the New Testament. Consequently, we must not read our own hope back into the Old Testament as if that were what the passages say (even when we can find brief glimpses of Gentile participation). Instead, we track the development to understand how our modern ideas have taken shape.

The Old Testament does not "prophesy" the transcendent hope, but the fulfillment identified in the New Testament reflects the repackaging of that literature to reflect the enhanced understanding that the ministry of Jesus affords (including incarnation and resurrection). The Israelites never see beyond the temporal bounds of the covenant. For them, the covenant is already/not yet in that they have it but have not realized its full potential. Christians have a sense of already/not yet regarding the kingdom of God, which arrived in the incarnation and the establishment of the church but has not yet reached the consummation that will come with the return of Christ.

Every culture has its conventional and traditional ways to describe normality—where everything is stable and one can enjoy an ordered life. Israelites would have expressed it as living under one's own vine and fig tree (1 Kings 4:25; Zech 3:10). In twenty-first-century North America it might be expressed the way I saw it recently in a book, where one of the characters whimsically wished for a nine-to-five job, a white picket fence, a black lab, and 2.5 kids. Notice how culturally embedded such descriptions are. This rather obtuse description of stable life in the United States would not be intuitively understood by other contemporary cultures (for example, Asian or African). It would not even have been understood by North Americans of the nineteenth century. Certainly, a culture five hundred years from now would be mystified by the description and would find it quite impenetrable.

It is therefore no surprise that when we encounter the culture of the Israelites in the Old Testament, or even the Greco-Roman Apocalypse of John, we have difficulty understanding the force of the descriptions of what would represent stability, order, and normality. That which they considered ideal used imagery and language as opaque to us as our descriptions would be to them. If identifying an ideal system today, we would often favor a democracy over a monarchy. Nevertheless, the biblical testimony for both Israel and the church features the latter. When we construct our eschatology, we will benefit most from an approach that takes both literary genre (for example, the nature of apocalyptic literature) and culture (such as ideas about ideal conditions) into account. Such considerations may result in a greater humility on our part: we don't know as much as we might think we do, and perhaps not as much as we would like to know. In this we are not unlike the prophets, who searched diligently to discover such things (1 Pet 1:10-11), or the disciples, who deeply desired to understand when the kingdom would come (Mt 24:3; Acts 1:6). Even the angels do not have access to such information (1 Pet 1:12).

Such humility may rightly caution us against all-too-frequent decoding attempts that often characterize our development of eschatological systems. Barton identifies the methodological dilemma in reference to the interpretation of Habakkuk found in the Qumran pesher:

> To extract such meanings requires the interpreter to treat the text as an elaborately coded message, in which none of the normal conventions of language and literature are relevant in establishing the sense: indeed, one might almost say that the text is no longer treated as a piece of continuous Hebrew at all, but as a cryptogram whose real meaning is, for the uninitiated, entirely veiled by the fact that it has a surface meaning which deflects the simple reader from guessing that there is anything mysterious about it.[6]

Should our interpretation reflect such approaches, it would undermine the very biblical authority, vested in the author's intentions, that we claim as being the foundation of our theology and our hope.

---

[6]Barton, *Oracles of God*, 182-83.

PART 5

APOCALYPTIC

Proposition 14

Apocalyptic Should Be Differentiated from Classical Prophecy

I begin with a lengthy quote that offers the insight of Lorenzo DiTommaso to set the stage not only for this proposition but for the unit.

> Apocalypticism is often mistaken for what it is not. It is not millennialism or utopianism, even though many apocalyptic groups are millennial in their outlook or utopian in their social agendas. It is not messianism or fundamentalism, even though apocalyptic literature regularly features messianic figures, and apocalyptic social movements can be fundamentalist in their attitudes. Apocalypticism is not eschatology, but it is eschatological, insofar as apocalyptic eschatology is one form of the study of the "last things." Nor is it the same as prophecy, conspiracy theory, or esotericism, even if for many people the notion of "apocalyptic" calls to mind the disclosure of hidden mysteries, the contrivance of secret plans, and the quest for arcane knowledge.[1]

I might add to his list of distinctions that apocalypticism is not about a battle between spiritual forces taking place in historical

---

[1]Lorenzo DiTommaso, "Apocalypticism and Popular Culture," in *Oxford Handbook of Apocalyptic Literature*, ed. John J. Collins (New York: Oxford University Press, 2014), 473-74.

spheres, providing the basis for what today can be called "conflict theology." It is true that spiritual forces occasionally make an appearance in apocalyptic, but I would contend that is not the defining feature. DiTommaso offers his own clarification that apocalypticism is "a distinctive combination of axioms or propositions about space, time, and human existence."[2] Perhaps this is a bit too general in that it neglects a specific reference to the religious nature of this perspective, particularly with regard to the expectation of the kingdom of God that is, arguably, the central tenet of at least its earliest exemplars.[3]

Given the challenges of a concise definition,[4] we should perhaps settle for a more extensive description. *Apocalyptic* is a scholarly category and one that can introduce problems because of its (differing) criteria regarding what should be counted as apocalyptic literature and what should not. Since the book of Revelation historically served as the baseline exemplar, some have worried that the label may orient the discussion prejudiciously toward Christianity (rather than Old Testament, ancient Near East, or Second Temple Judaism). And in

---

[2]DiTommaso, "Apocalypticism and Popular Culture," 474. I should note that it is becoming more commonplace in this area of scholarship to contend there is no such thing as apocalyptic*ism*, but that is an argument for another place and time.

[3]Admittedly, modern apocalypses can often be entirely secular (cf. *The Matrix* and many other productions imagining a dystopic post-apocalyptic reality) or simply portend the end of the world as we know it (cf. the Mayan calendar apocalypse). Both of these and numerous others are discussed in DiTommaso's article.

[4]The most commonly cited definition was introduced in John J. Collins, ed., *Apocalypse: The Morphology of a Genre*, Semeia 14 (Atlanta: Society of Biblical Literature, 1979), 9. As revised by Adela Yarbro Collins, "Introduction," in *Early Christian Apocalypticism: Genre and Social Setting*, ed. Adela Yarbro Collins, Semeia 36 (Philadelphia: Society of Biblical Literature, 1986), 7, it reads,

> a genre of revelatory literature with a narrative framework, in which a revelation is mediated by an otherworldly being to a human recipient, disclosing a transcendent reality which is both temporal, insofar as it envisages eschatological salvation, and spatial insofar as it involves another, supernatural world intended to interpret present, earthly circumstances in light of the supernatural world and of the future, and to influence both the understanding and the behavior of the audience by means of divine authority.

Nevertheless, though it is cited often, it is also regularly criticized on one account or another. Consequently, it stands only as a starting point for the discussion, not a reflection of the scholarly status quo.

fact the application of the term to an academic literary category does have nineteenth-century Christian roots. Yet, it should be recognized that even good labels are heuristic—that is, they serve a purpose for expediting discussion—but they can also quickly be recognized as reductionistic. Labels can be helpful as differentiators, caution signs against imposing ideas of one area onto another (for example, assuming that apocalyptic is prophetic). But labels can also artificially restrict. Labels can help identify discontinuity between categories but can also lead to obscuring important elements of continuity.

Apocalyptic describes a category of literature (in contrast to prophecy, an institution that is often oral). I have already noted that *apocalyptic* can be described as one stage within the development of how people have thought about communication from the divine. I have traced the general stages beginning with preclassical prophecy, where Israelites such as Deborah, Samuel, Nathan, and Elijah served the leadership of the people (as prophets throughout the ancient Near East did).

Classical prophecy is the next stage and dominates the Hebrew Bible (see table 14.1). It features spoken oracles that are heavily covenant focused. These are eventually compiled into the books in our Bibles. Classical prophecy continues into the postexilic period, though in somewhat altered form as it more often describes a present judgment rather than a coming judgment.

The next stage is where apocalyptic fits in, as new communicative methods (for example, visions) become more prominent, and the scope expands beyond the covenant as it shifts its focus to God's plans and purposes for universal world history. Continuity is found as this continues to be received as divine communication. The primary message of apocalyptic is for the people to persevere. This stands in contrast to classical prophecy, where the call was to return to the covenant.

Table 14.1. Comparison of classical prophecy and Jewish apocalyptic literature

CLASSICAL PROPHECY IN THE HEBREW BIBLE	JEWISH APOCALYPTIC
Direct divine revelation ("Thus says the Lord")	Mediated revelation through visions or heavenly beings
Word from God to be proclaimed	Vision from God to be understood
Prophet speaks oracles	Visionary records the vision and its interpretation
Oracles that claim to reproduce the speech of God directly	Revelatory visions that claim to unveil mysteries about the past, present, and future
Projects a plan for Israel's history	Projects a pattern of universal history
Driven by indictment leading to restoration	Driven by pattern leading to kingdom of God
Rooted in time and history	Transcends time and history with cosmic scope
Exhortation to return to covenant faithfulness: reverse course	Exhortation to be faithful to the covenant in crisis: steady on
Ethical urgency for changing course of events	Reflects a level of historical determinism
Projects the consequences of Israel's covenant failures rooted in the blessings and curses of the covenant	Projects a certain kind of future, rooted in the patterns of the past, to reorient readers' thinking about the present
Focus on God's rule over Israel established by the covenant	Focus on God's rule over the kingdoms of the world
Announces exile (offenses leading to it, result of judgment, restoration coming from it)	Resolves exile (kings and empires are transitory)
Divine judgment leads to salvation or destruction in this world	Extends the timeline of divine judgment to include post mortem judgment for the wicked and reward for the righteous.

Source: Aubrey E. Buster and John H. Walton, *The Book of Daniel*, New International Commentary on the Old Testament (Grand Rapids, MI: Eerdmans, forthcoming).

One of the features of continuity between classical prophecy and apocalyptic is the concept of order. Classical prophecy, with its focus on the covenant, is inherently concerned with Israel. The covenant was God's mechanism for providing for order within Israel. The covenant provided for relationship between Israel and Yahweh. It was informed through Torah, which illustrated what order would look like, and it provided for the establishment of Yahweh's presence on earth—he who is the center and source of order.[5] Apocalyptic literature also has its primary focus on order, a centrality well expressed by Carol Newsom:

[5]I have engaged in further discussion of these connections in John H. Walton and J. Harvey Walton, *The Lost World of the Torah* (Downers Grove, IL: IVP Academic, 2019), as well as in John H. Walton, *Old Testament Theology for Christians* (Downers Grove, IL: IVP Academic, 2017).

Although the content of the revealed knowledge found in apocalypses is varied, it is overwhelmingly concerned with the discernment of patterns of order. This order may be cosmological, historical, or moral. Order is at the heart of the symbolic imagination of apocalyptic literature and shapes its rhetoric.[6]

She finds evidences in the attention given to the movements of the heavens, the hierarchies among heavenly beings, mathematical symbols, the calendar with its focus on time, the periodization of history, and the quest for moral order in times of crisis and oppression. Collins notes further that numbers are routinely used since they represent the ways in which time is ordered.[7]

Apocalyptic literature has potential roots in the ancient Near East, though no clear precursors can be identified—only certain select characteristics (see table 14.3). The genre proper becomes most evident in the Hellenistic period, from the earliest commonly accepted exemplar in the third century BC to its pervasive presence from the second century BC through the second century AD, first in Jewish circles, then in Christian literature (see table 14.2).[8]

---

[6]Carol A. Newsom, "The Rhetoric of Jewish Apocalyptic Literature," in Collins, *Oxford Handbook of Apocalyptic Literature,* 212.

[7]Adela Yarbro Collins, *Cosmology and Eschatology in Jewish and Christian Apocalypses* (Leiden: Brill, 1996), 90, 135-38.

[8]The extent of this list is debatable. James H. Charlesworth, ed., *The Old Testament Pseudepigrapha,* 2 vols. (Garden City, NY: Doubleday, 1983–1985), provides an anthology of texts. In his first volume, he includes over a dozen pieces. For the Jewish pieces, I have included here only the major exemplars, taking my lead from Daniel M. Gurtner, *Introducing the Pseudepigrapha of Second Temple Judaism* (Grand Rapids, MI: Baker Academic, 2020). Different lists occur depending on which features are considered essential to the definition. (That is, some determinations are made based on otherworldly journeys or the presence of visions; others are based on historical overview of the past as future, and still others on the periodization of history.) Other possible features include angelic visitations, historical determinism, cosmic battles, judgment of the righteous and wicked, and mythological imagery. The list of Christian apocalypses generally includes twenty to twenty-four pieces. Lists and discussion can be found in Collins, *Apocalypse.*

Table 14.2. Select list of apocalyptic literature outside the Bible

WORK	DATE	FEATURES*				JEWISH/ CHRISTIAN
		OW	SV	HO	PH	
Book of the Watchers (1 Enoch 1–36)	3rd/2nd c. BC	X	X			Jewish
Sibylline Oracles (books 3–5)	3rd/2nd c. BC		X	X	X	Jewish
Animal Apocalypse (1 Enoch 85–90)	2nd c. BC		X	X	X	Jewish
Apocalypse of Weeks (1 Enoch 93:1-10; 91:11-17)	2nd c. BC				X	Jewish
Messianic Apocalypse (4Q521)	2nd c. BC					Jewish (Qumran)
11QMelchizedek (11Q13)	1st c. BC				X	Jewish (Qumran)
Aramaic Apocalypse (4Q246)	1st c. BC		?			Jewish (Qumran)
Apocryphon of Jeremiah (4Q387)	1st c. BC			X	X	Jewish (Qumran)
2 Enoch	1st c. AD	X	X			Jewish
4 Ezra	1st c. AD		X	X	X	Jewish
2 Baruch	1st c. AD		X		X	Jewish
Gabriel Revelation	1st c. BC / 1st c. AD		X			Jewish
Testament of Abraham	1st c. AD	X	X		X	Jewish?
Shepherd of Hermas		?	X		X	Christian
Ascension of Isaiah			X			Christian
Apocalypse of Zephaniah	2nd c. AD	X	X			Jewish?
Apocalypse of Peter	2nd c. AD	X	X			Christian
Sibylline Oracles (books 1–2, 6–7)	2nd/3rd c. AD			X		Christian?
Apocalypse of Paul	4th c. AD	X	X			Christian
Apocalypse of Thomas	2nd–4th c. BC		X	?	?	Christian

*Major features: OW = otherworldly journey; SV = symbolic visions; HO = historical overview of past as future; PH = periodization of history

   Apocalyptic literature can be viewed as distilling contributions from outside Judaism (Egyptian, Akkadian, Zoroastrianism, and Hellenism) combined with long-standing literary traditions of the Hebrew Bible (prophetic literature and Wisdom literature in general and Ezekiel and Zechariah in particular). We can observe some of the similarities with various cultural and literary tributaries, but tracing what could be called contributions or influences is much more hypothetical. Apocalyptic literature nevertheless stands as a distinguishable literary entity even as it blends into its surroundings and overlaps with them in numerous ways.[9] One of the most important differences between these tributary works and Jewish apocalyptic is that these are generally limited in their vision to the culture in which they were written rather than pertaining to world history.

Table 14.3. Possible tributaries to apocalyptic literature

WORK	DATE	FEATURES*				CULTURE
		OW	SV	HO	PH	
Prophecies of Neferti	20th c. BC			?		Egyptian
Admonitions of Ipuwer	18th c. BC					Egyptian
Marduk Speech	12th c. BC			X		Babylonian
Shulgi Speech	12th c. BC		X	?		Babylonian
Text A	12th c. BC			?		Babylonian
Dynastic Prophecy	4th c. BC			?		Babylonian
Uruk Text	3rd c. BC			?		Babylonian
Demotic Chronicle	4th/3rd c. BC		?	X	X	Egyptian
Oracle of the Lamb	3rd/2nd c. BC					Egyptian
Dream of Nectanebo	2nd c. BC		X			Egyptian
Oracle of the Potter	2nd c. AD fragments; origins 2nd c. BC?					Egyptian
Zand-ī Wahman Yašn	Earliest copy 9th c. AD; origins Hellenistic?	X	?	X		Persian

*Major features: OW = otherworldly journey; SV = symbolic visions; HO = historical overview of past as future; PH = periodization of history

Source: Discussions can be found in Matthew Neujahr, *Predicting the Past in the Ancient Near East: Mantic Historiography in Ancient Mesopotamia, Judah, and the Mediterranean World*, Brown Judaic Studies 354 (Providence, RI: Brown Judaic Studies, 2012); Kenton L. Sparks, *Ancient Texts for the Study of the Hebrew Bible* (Peabody, MA: Hendrickson, 2005), 240-51; Tawny L. Holm, *Of Courtiers and Kings: The Biblical Daniel Narratives and Ancient Story-Collections* (Winona Lake, IN: Eisenbrauns, 2013), 387-414; and John J. Collins, *Apocalypticism in the Dead Sea Scrolls* (New York: Routledge, 1997).

Besides using the medium of visions with symbolic components, apocalyptic literature prominently features the identification of historical patterns and a sense of historical determinism. These features

---

[9]Adapted from Aubrey E. Buster and John H. Walton, *The Book of Daniel*, New International Commentary on the Old Testament (Grand Rapids, MI: Eerdmans, forthcoming). Najman refers to this as a constellation of features and precursors. Hindy Najman, *Losing the Temple and Recovering the Future: An Analysis of 4 Ezra* (New York: Cambridge University Press, 2014), 20-23.

clarify the purpose of apocalyptic literature. It looks at the past to develop patterns and then extends those patterns into the future. Consequently, this literature deals with trajectories. As in geometry, when connecting two points allows extending the line into an infinite future, so apocalyptic has connected some dots in the past and tracked them into a future that the vector can be seen as projecting.

Apocalyptic does not have the purpose of foretelling the future. Instead, it reveals how God's plans and purposes begun in the past will find future completion; it projects a pattern. For those who hold to the inspired nature of particular apocalyptic texts, it is this identification of the pattern that is inspired. By tracking the course of the pattern, the future takes on a predetermined shape, at least on the larger scale. This stands in contrast to the open-ended conditionality that often characterized prophecy. In apocalyptic literature, the fulfillment does not take sudden course changes as can be found at times in prophecy (for example, Jonah's Nineveh). Instead, the future is constantly taking new shape along the same vector as visions are interpreted and adopted as they intertwine with the unfolding events of history.

Proposition 15

In Apocalyptic Literature, Visions Are Not the Message but the Occasion for the Message

The exotic symbolism of apocalyptic literature can easily prompt readers to creative strategies for connecting the dots in such a way that attention is drawn to the unfolding events of the readers' day. As equations are the currency of mathematics, symbols can be considered the currency of apocalyptic visions. Given this stock in trade, it is incumbent on the interpreter to decide how the symbols should be approached. Symbols are characterized by having two aspects to their meaning—the thing in itself and the thing that it stands for. In Daniel, for example, the symbol is the horn, and it stands for a king. They often have traditional roots in literature and culture. However, they should not be treated as ciphers to be decoded. When we encounter them in apocalyptic texts, we should be investigating not just what they represent but what cultural significance may be contributing meaning to the representation.[1]

In this proposition I will focus mainly on the visions of Daniel since those are the clearest and most extensive examples of apocalyptic

---

[1] Adapted from Aubrey E. Buster and John H. Walton, *The Book of Daniel*, New International Commentary on the Old Testament (Grand Rapids, MI: Eerdmans, forthcoming).

literature in the Old Testament. The text of Daniel gives us every confidence that, in that context, the symbols of beasts and horns stand for
kings and their kingdoms. The text itself identifies the symbols in this
way, and we can adopt this meaning without hesitation. We should
have less confidence when we attempt to suggest which kingdoms are
represented. The book of Daniel gives clear indication that Babylon is
the first (Dan 2; 7). Subsequently, Daniel 8 identifies the two animal
protagonists as Persia and Greece, signifying two more empires,
though it is up for debate which two.

When it comes to identifying the three ribs in the bear's mouth, the
four heads of the leopard, or the ten horns of the fourth beast, we possess
no textual indicators for identification. The symbolism may well have
been transparent to contemporary readers, but even early in the history
of interpretation there was no consensus on what the symbols mean or
refer to. The symbols may also have clear referents (for example, horns =
kings) without indicating a clear fulfillment (which kings?). Other times,
as in the case of the three ribs in the bear's mouth, the referent is opaque
and in fact may not even exist. It is possible that the three ribs pertain
to three political entities, but, alternatively, portraying ribs in the bear's
mouth offers a certain imagery (devouring) that thereby has meaning
even if the elements have no specific referents.

Our proposition makes the important differentiation between the
vision and the message so that we can avoid confusing the two. It may
not need to be said, but readers should not expect that the interactions
in the visions will someday be reality. We would expect neither to see
beasts arising from the sea (Dan 7) nor to observe a ram and a goat
having a butting contest in Iran (Dan 8). We would not engage in a
stakeout at a myrtle grove waiting for a company of horsemen riding
different-colored horses (Zech 1) or be on the lookout for a woman
riding a scarlet beast (Rev 17). In the same manner, we would not
expect to see the Lamb on Mount Zion with 144,000 saints (Rev 14)
or the rider on the white horse (Rev 19).

A major aspect of the symbolism used in visions is found in numbers. Yet their role in the message may not be strictly numerical. Once we recognize this, we will be less concerned with trying to calculate the details of, for example, the seventy sevens (Dan 9:24, further discussed later in this proposition) or the 1,290 days (Dan 12:11) or to penetrate the meaning of 666 (Rev 13:18) as if these were simply numerical values. In symbolism, there is always more going on than meets the eye.

The message found in the visions of Daniel focuses on the arrival of the kingdom of God. The visions provide the *occasion* for the message of this literature. The messages themselves are set forth clearly; they are not mystical or opaque, and their understanding is not dependent on specific identification of the symbols. For example, regardless of which beasts represent which kingdoms or which horns equal which kings, they all stand under condemnation and will be swept away by the kingdom of God. Similarly, regardless of when one considers the seventieth seven (often understood as a week of years) of Daniel to take place, it will witness the end of the oppressor and the rise of God's people.

We can consider as an example the question of the ten horns in Daniel 7. First, I will reiterate a point I have already made: to understand the message, we need to know only that the ten horns represent ten kings, and the text tells us that (Dan 7:24). We do not need to know which ten kings they are. The readers of Daniel in the second century BC, living prior to the rise of Rome (and, soon after that, of Christianity), would have seen the fourth kingdom (in which the ten horns occur) as the Hellenistic kingdom of the Seleucids and would have identified the ten horns from that swath of history.

After the Seleucids had passed into the pages of history, however, Rome was an obvious replacement choice as the fourth kingdom.[2] This

---

[2]It is of interest that in 2 Esdras 12:10-12 (dated to AD 90), Ezra specifically identifies the view of the fourth kingdom being Rome as one that differed from what his "brother" Daniel had seen.

modification in interpretation illustrates what the history of interpretation demonstrates: the power of the visions is found in their flexibility; they can be adapted and recontextualized by endless generations of interpreters. The four-kingdom model itself was sufficiently pliable that invested readers from various time periods backfilled it with their history and from the perspective of their moment in time.[3] In repeated circumstances, the message is rebirthed to console people of God living in troubled times to recognize that the world's kings and kingdoms will all pass away. It is common for people to believe that they live in the time of the fourth kingdom and that therefore the kingdom of God is at hand.[4]

The discussion of the identity of the ten horns is infinitely more complicated. Multiple possibilities exist for identifying them in any given period of interpretation.[5] In the aftermath of the death of Alexander the Great, candidates for inclusion could vary decade by decade as power centers shifted and new players came on the scene. Different interpreters would have made different identifications. One option is to consider them sequential;[6] another is to see them in a snapshot of the array of political powers at a certain time. For example, after the death of Alexander, the Greek kingdom was theoretically divided among four of his generals, but other contenders for power joined the field. Besides the four generals (Antigonus One-Eye,

---

[3]For documentation of this reception history see Brennan W. Breed, "Daniel's Four Kingdoms Schema: A History of Re-writing World History," *Interpretation* 71, no. 2 (2017): 178-89.
[4]Some today might associate the fourth kingdom with Russia, or with Europe, or even with the United States. This is exactly the point—we can only guess. But the fourth kingdom generates terror, while the expectation of the kingdom of God nurtures hope.
[5]I presented one possible scheme within the Hellenistic setting many years ago to demonstrate the feasibility of such a perspective: John H. Walton, "Daniel's Four Kingdoms," *Journal of the Evangelical Theological Society* 29, no. 1 (1986): 25-36.
[6]In fact, a Babylonian list of Macedonian kings featuring ten rulers from Alexander the Great leading up to Antiochus IV is in the holdings of the British Museum. Its list is Alexander the Great, Philip III Arrhidaios, Alexander IV, Seleucus I, Antiochus I, Antiochus II, Seleucus II, Seleucus III, Antiochus III, Seleucus IV. Publication in Jean-Jacques Glassner, *Mesopotamian Chronicles*, ed. Benjamin R. Foster, Writings from the Ancient World 19 (Atlanta: Society of Biblical Literature, 2004), 134-37.

Lysimachus, Antipater, and Ptolemy), between the years of 323 and 320 BC six additional power players would include Perdiccas (Alexander's regent), Philip III (half brother of Alexander), Alexander IV (infant son of Alexander the Great), Demetrius (son of Antigonus), Cassander (son of Antipater), and Seleucus (Satrap of Babylon). If, alternatively, one thinks of kingdoms rather than those who would be kings, we could note that by the end of the third century BC what had been Alexander's empire had become ten independent kingdoms: Ptolemaic Egypt, Seleucia, Macedon, Pergamum, Pontus, Bithynia, Cappadocia, Armenia, Parthia, and Bactria.[7]

I am not claiming that any of these potential lists of ten are the "right" identifications. They demonstrate only that numerous plausible identifications could easily be made prior to the Roman period. Both Christian and Jewish interpreters eventually adopted Rome as the fourth kingdom. This is no surprise since the Hellenistic kingdoms had shriveled without the arrival of the kingdom of God (in the political shape of their current expectations). Such disappointments led inevitably to countless recalibrations. When, after the fall of Rome (whenever one posits that), the kingdom of God failed to materialize, other strategies were found, including the idea of the reconstructed Roman Empire that features prominently in modern end-time schemes. As would be expected, even these schemes propose different identifications of this reconstructed group of ten, which include possibilities such as the United Nations, the European Union, or NATO, to name just a few.[8] There is no need for such identifications, and they provide no confidence.

If anyone can generate their own list, we are left with nothing but ever-changing opinions. The authority is in the message, not in our decoding of the symbols or their referents. And the message is clear:

---

[7]For details, see Walton, "Daniel's Four Kingdoms," 32-33.
[8]For elaboration and discussion see Amy Johnson Frykholm, "Apocalypticism in Contemporary Christianity," in *The Oxford Handbook of Apocalyptic Literature*, ed. John J. Collins (New York: Oxford University Press, 2014), 441-56.

the kingdoms of this world will prevail for a time through many seasons, but the kingdom of God will overcome and endure forever.[9] In general terms, God's order will be established as represented in his kingdom. We should be content with that as our hope.

All of this illustrates the point that the symbols (here, beasts and the horns) *do* represent something tangible in the message, but we do not need to move beyond what the text actually tells us about those symbols to understand what the message is. That is, the message is clear even when the identification of the referents is uncertain or has multiple options.

Finally, then, we need to address how apocalyptic does or does not provide a foundation for end-time eschatology. I believe that it is for the good of the church to acknowledge that apocalyptic does *not* provide such a foundation. Marvin Pate summarizes the situation well when, talking about the book of Revelation, he concludes, "Such a crystal ball reading of the last book in the Bible, however, has undoubtedly caused more harm than good and is best avoided by responsible hermeneuticians."[10] I have seven reasons (an appropriate number!) supporting my conviction that we should not be engaged in building such systems.

1. It is not essential to devise an eschatological system to make sense of apocalyptic. This literature can be understood as offering interpretation of the events that were unfolding in its contemporary setting. Recontextualization is always possible, but it is not necessary. The message of apocalyptic is nonetheless clear—the kingdom of God will be established.

---

[9]Even the number four may be symbolic here since four-kingdom schemes were the convention characteristic of periodizations in numerous cultures. See Buster and Walton, *Book of Daniel*, forthcoming. Extensive treatment of numerical symbolism and its associations and manifestations in Second Temple Judaism can be found in Adela Yarbro Collins, *Cosmology and Eschatology in Jewish and Christian Apocalypses* (Leiden: Brill, 1996), 55-138.

[10]C. Marvin Pate, ed., introduction to *Four Views on the Book of Revelation* (Grand Rapids, MI: Zondervan, 1998), 9.

2. Consequently, apocalyptic literature is functional and can be interpreted plausibly without requiring an end-times fulfillment. The kingdom of God is coming. It is true that interpreters may find their own circumstances to resonate with apocalyptic scenarios, but that is insufficient to devise timelines regarding the "biblical" view of the end times.

3. Understanding the message of apocalyptic is not dependent on imagining events that will shape the future. If, as I have contended, the authority of the text is found in the message intended by the author, then our systems and timelines do not carry authority, and they should therefore be of less interest to us.

4. If our hope is properly related to the authoritative message, it is, by definition, not dependent on our attempts to construct an eschatology.

5. The history of the church bears witness to the incontrovertible fact that eschatological systems divide the church. The mission of the church is to make disciples, to bring honor to the name of God/Christ, and to be his people in a troubled world. When we are arguing among ourselves about eschatological systems, we easily get distracted from our mission.[11]

6. Eschatological systems and predictions have a checkered history. When we place our confidence in such things, it does not strengthen our faith but potentially weakens it because when formulated expectations do not materialize, some (whether inside the church or looking on from the outside) conclude that the Bible cannot be trusted or is not true.

7. Perhaps most tragically, our eschatological disputes, claims, and systems can easily bring disrepute on the name of God, on the

---

[11]This can happen with other theological issues as well, but that does not undermine the point. Also, note that I am not suggesting that just because points are controversial and disputed does not mean that they are not important.

Bible, and on his people. When outsiders scoff at our systems and predictions, we cannot conclude that we are being persecuted for the sake of the gospel—eschatological systems should not be mistaken for the gospel. Moreover, it is Christ crucified that is a stumbling block to the outside world (1 Cor 1:23). Our eschatological systems should not be posing such a stumbling block.

My conclusion, then, is that apocalyptic literature cannot and should not be used as a foundation for constructing eschatological systems, timelines, and predictions. Recognition of its genre and context is sufficient to understand its powerful message, as stated in the last proposition, that God's people are to persevere because the kingdom of God is coming. Though it is always possible that the future will unfold in patterns similar to what we find in apocalyptic literature (reflected in a higher sense of historical determinism), those patterns do not determine the details of the future; they only offer glimpses of God's purposes as a work in process. This still leaves us the question of Daniel's seventy weeks, the most central apocalyptic piece to eschatological puzzles, to which I now turn in the following excursus.

EXCURSUS: TECHNICAL STUDY
OF DANIEL'S SEVENTY WEEKS OF YEARS

It would not be an overstatement to suggest that the seventy-weeks prophecy is one of the core passages used today when discussing eschatology and formulating various eschatological paradigms. Readers are faced with many puzzling questions as they read Daniel 9:24-27. What is the word that goes forth (Dan 9:25)? Is it a prophetic word? If so, whose? Or is it a royal decree? If so, which one? What is the distinguishing characteristic of the "end" (Dan 9:26-27)? Does it refer to the end of a particular time period? The end of a ruler? The end of a crisis? If both the starting point and the ending point are uncertain, and we do not know how the intervals were calculated to get

from one to the other (for example, are regular ad hoc intercalations[a] to be counted?), we are left without an objective way to do straightforward calculations.

Consequently, most interpreters throughout history have begun by deciding who they believe the anointed one(s) is (are) (the Hebrew word for "anointed one" is *mashiah*), and then applying the numbers to arrive at some correspondence to historical events. Given all the questions about calculating the time span that I have noted, the numbers cannot be used as an objective guide to reveal the identity of the anointed one(s). Instead, the numbers and calendar system have to be tailored to defend the proposed identification. In that case, an interpretive preconception about fulfillment is driving the analysis rather than the details given by the author in the text.

As I now turn attention to the identification of the anointed one(s), I begin by noting my unqualified acceptance of the idea that ultimately, Jesus is *the* Anointed One, the Messiah, the Christ. Nevertheless, that does not resolve the question whether Jesus is the anointed one Daniel 9 refers to because many anointed ones can be identified both in Israelite history and in the biblical text.[b]

In Daniel 9, the Hebrew text speaks of *an* anointed one (twice, see ESV), not *the* Anointed One (as in NIV). It is not immediately clear whether the two references to an anointed one in Daniel 9:25-26 are speaking of the same person or of two different people. Do they both refer to Jesus? Or perhaps just one of them does? The audience that was experiencing some fulfillment of Daniel's vision in the second century BC likely already recognized those anointed ones as signposts along the way to the seventieth week, through which that audience would have believed they were living.

The question about whether the passage is speaking of the same anointed one twice or of two different anointed ones separated by centuries can be approached by comparing the NIV translation to that found in the ESV. The NIV reads,[c]

> Know and understand this: From the time the word goes out to restore and rebuild Jerusalem until the Anointed One, the ruler, comes, there will be seven "sevens," and sixty-two "sevens." It will be rebuilt with streets and a trench, but in times of trouble. After the sixty-two "sevens," the Anointed

> One will be put to death and will have nothing. (Dan 9:25-26)

Of importance here is that in Daniel 9:25 the seven sevens is combined with the sixty-two sevens, which is then followed by punctuation indicating a hard stop (period). The result is that the two references to the anointed one can be understood to be to the same individual, who would come after sixty-nine weeks (a sum never referred to in the text). Note also that the translators capitalize "Anointed One" (interpretive since Hebrew has no capital letters) and that they supply the definite article *the* in front of each, though the Hebrew text does not use the definite article here. In this way, the reader is given an interpretive, and potentially prejudicial, view of identity by the translator's choices.

The ESV translation demonstrates a different set of choices:[d]

> Know therefore and understand that from the going out of the word to restore and build Jerusalem to the coming of an anointed one, a prince, there shall be seven weeks. Then for sixty-two weeks it shall be built again with squares and moat, but in a troubled time. And after the sixty-two weeks, an anointed one shall be cut off and shall have nothing. (Dan 9:25-26 ESV)

Here the punctuation (period) is placed after "seven weeks." Consequently, a time period of sixty-two weeks separates the first anointed one from the second, suggesting that they are two different individuals. Moreover, these translators do not capitalize "anointed one," and, additionally, they reflect the indefiniteness of the Hebrew text ("an" anointed one). The ESV translation, which I prefer in this case because it does indeed represent the Hebrew Masoretic Text in these verses more faithfully, makes it much more difficult to conclude that it is talking about Jesus. I will first discuss the history of interpretation linking the passage to Jesus, then address this question: If the two anointed ones are centuries apart, who are they, and what is their significance?

Since the second century AD, Christian interpretation has been almost unanimous in reading this passage as prophesying Jesus.[e] Among the most extensive modern defenses of this interpretation was that presented by Harold Hoehner.[f] In his view, the sixty-nine weeks (seven + sixty-two) extend from the decree of Artaxerxes in 445 (permitting Nehemiah to return to rebuild Jerusalem) until the triumphal entry of Christ (which he dates to March 30 [Nisan 10], AD 33, a highly debatable pinpointing).[g] This position is very popular among evangelicals and is often used in apologetics.

Hoehner, and those who accept his view, have begun with the assumption that Jesus *is* the Messiah (with which, theologically, I have no argument) but proceed with the assumption that any reference to a future, unnamed, "anointed one" (such as here in Daniel) *must* find its fulfillment in Jesus since he is the one through whom the kingdom of God came. It is significant to note that the New Testament never suggests that Jesus should be understood as the anointed one to whom Daniel 9 points.[h]

Christian readers are often unaware that in the Old Testament the term *mashiaḥ* has not yet become the primary descriptor for the future, ideal, Davidic king.[i] In light of this realization, Daniel 9 can be understood to feature messianic (= anointed) figures (broadly defined), but that does not mean it contains a messianic *theology*. (For example, in Dan 9, messiah is neither a warrior, nor a

judge, nor a king; is not Davidic; and does not bring restoration.) In fact, such a specific messianic theology is absent from all the early apocalypses.[j]

Now we can turn attention to the alternative, that two separate anointed ones are indicated and that neither of them is Jesus. This interpretation is widely held today in both confessional and nonconfessional circles, but many variations remain concerning who the two individuals might be. Among the earliest attestations to this interpretive option is the Old Greek translation of the Old Testament, which predates Christianity. There, the passage is clarified to indicate that it refers to the second century BC. The translators date the events of Daniel 9:26 after 7 + 70 + 62 weeks, which they specify as referring to the 139th year of the Seleucid era, which was about 172 BC.[k]

The most common interpretation is that the anointed ones are, respectively, the Persian king Cyrus and Onias III, the Jewish high priest who was murdered in 171 BC. In Isaiah 45:1, Cyrus is identified as "anointed," so we can acknowledge that he was well known in that role to a Jewish audience. It is not difficult to calculate that he arrives after the first seven weeks of years since any number of starting points in Daniel 9:25 could lead to significant events in the career of Cyrus forty-nine years later.[l]

With regard to Onias III, in the second century much intrigue surrounded the priesthood since the high priest was the highest Jewish official in the land. In the time of the Seleucid king, Antiochus IV Epiphanes, the priesthood was sold on a number of occasions, eventually to one without the traditional (Zadokite) priestly lineage. Onias III, the anointed high priest, was the last legitimate Zadokite priest.

His murder was one of the central events for the Jews of the second century, as evidenced from its prominent role in the contemporary books of the history of this period, 1 and 2 Maccabees. Most intriguingly, the time span between the beginning of the exile (605 in Daniel's context, Dan 1:1), and the death of Onias III in 171 is 434 years (sixty-two sevens). Furthermore, the death of Onias III could easily be seen as the beginning of the seven-year period that ended with the rededication of the desecrated altar in 164 BC. This would constitute the seventieth week. At this point, the second-century Jewish audience would expect nothing further—Daniel's timetable had been fulfilled.[m]

Nevertheless, numerous alternatives to Cyrus have been suggested as the first anointed one, and certainty is impossible. I am intrigued by the proposal that Joshua, the high priest of the return, would be a strong candidate.[n] Joshua is a contemporary of Cyrus, so the chronology would be similar. He provides an attractive alternative to Cyrus in that he would parallel Onias III, both being anointed priests (for this explicitly stated about Joshua, see Zech 4:14; cf. Zech 3). Like most interpreters, my decision about the identity of the anointed ones precedes the decisions about the time periods. Though the identity of the anointed one(s) is the most pressing issue, many other factors can affect interpretation, including

1. Is Daniel presenting a precise chronology or a chronography? A chronography is a rhetorically driven adaptation involving patterning of time, such as Jubilee Years. Chronography incorporates historical referents into a symbolic structure (rather than a purely chronological sequence) with political and/or theological implications.[o] The Jews favored a Jubilee-heptadic chronography that configured periods of time and patterns in history according to Sabbatical Years and the periods of forty-nine years between Jubilee Years, based on Leviticus 25. Daniel 9 could be seen to reflect this sort of chronography as its 490 years equals both seventy sevens (heptadic) and ten Jubilees (49 x 10).[p] If this period of time represents a chronography, we cannot simply do the math.

2. What calendar is being used? The Seleucids and the Jews in the second century BC had competing calendars.[q]

3. What is the starting point? Many have considered it to be a king's decree (often Artaxerxes), while others have proposed that it is the prophetic word of Jeremiah (Jer 25:12-14; 29:4-14). A third alternative is that it refers to a decree from the heavenly council.

4. If the end point is Jesus, what event in Jesus' life is referred to, and how well can we pinpoint exact dates of that event?

5. What is the significance of the division of the time period into 7 + 62 + 1?

These are all complicated issues and cannot be treated in any detail in a book of this sort.[r] Nevertheless, the very nature and extent of these questions can provide the basis for exercising necessary caution.

At this point, I can only offer some of the conclusions I have provisionally adopted. I contend that Daniel's seventy weeks do pertain to the "end" *in the time frame of the book of Daniel*, which is fully addressed in the second-century BC context of the book. It is defensible to view the anointed ones as the priests, Joshua and Onias III, who serve as signposts in a Jewish chronography. The seventieth week in this view would be the persecution of Antiochus IV Epiphanes, and the end is the end of Seleucid dominion.

Finally, I return to the fact that neither Jesus nor the Evangelists nor Paul ever connects the dots between Jesus and the seventy weeks—and they could have done so any number of times. If Jesus *were* the anointed one who was cut off, why does the New Testament never make that observation? If the 490 leads us to him, that would be significant for those Gospel writers eager to show how Jesus fulfilled prophecy. When the calculations are only our own, we need to consider how central they should be in our interpretation. History is littered with the failed theories (or cults) that relied too heavily on eschatological predictions based on Daniel 9. As Haydon affirms, "Our place in this storyline demands we take care in our study of the end-times and not subtract from such a glorious hope by giving in to our predilection for cheap talk concerning the last days."[5] Our interpretation and proclamation of God's word through Daniel should reflect such a perspective. We respond properly to Daniel by exercising wisdom, enduring to the end, faithful through times of crisis.

Early in the history of interpretation of Daniel, Jerome warned,

> By breaking away from the stream of the past and directing his longing toward the future, [Apollinarius] very unsafely ventured an opinion concerning matters so obscure. If by any chance those of future generations should not see these predictions of his fulfilled at the time he set, then they will be forced to seek for some other solutions and to convict the teacher himself of erroneous interpretation.[t]

Sound advice. Hippolytus, the author of the earliest extant Christian biblical commentary (AD 200), and centuries before Jerome,

suggested that circumspect readers would do well to avoid inquiring about when the expected events will occur, instead having faith that they will indeed occur.[u]

---

[a]*Intercalations* refers to the ancient practice of occasionally adding extra months to bring the lunar and solar calendars into compliance. In modern times we accomplish this by adding an extra day to February every four years. In the ancient world, the timing or regularity of such intercalations was not predetermined and was at times controversial.

[b]Kings, prophets, and priests generally are all offices filled by anointed ones, and individuals such as Cyrus are so identified (Is 45:1).

[c]The same decisions are reflected in KJV, NASB, and NLT.

[d]The same approach is reflected in NRSV, NCB, and CEB.

[e]Perhaps the earliest being Julius Africanus (160–240), who indicated that the seventy sevens cover the period from the appointment of Nehemiah until the death of Christ. Jerome, *Commentary on Daniel* 15, indicates that Daniel spoke more plainly of Christ than any of the other prophets in that he "set forth the very time at which He would come." Jerome's commentary is translated by Gleason L. Archer, accessible electronically at www.tertullian.org/fathers/jerome_daniel_02_text.htm.

[f]Harold W. Hoehner, *Chronological Aspects of the Life of Christ* (Grand Rapids, MI: Zondervan, 1977). His calculations are comparable to those of Sir Robert Anderson, *The Coming Prince* (1894; repr., Grand Rapids, MI: Kregel, 1972), though he tweaks some of Anderson's data. Anderson (1841–1918) was not a biblical scholar but an investigator with Scotland Yard.

[g]Hoehner, *Chronological Aspects*, 138. This is based on his calculation using years of 360 days, thus arriving at a total time of 173,855 days, which he then converts to the modern calendar. One of the drawbacks of this is that it cannot include intercalations.

[h]Ron Haydon, *"Seventy Sevens Are Decreed": A Canonical Approach to Daniel 9:24-27* (Winona Lake, IN: Eisenbrauns, 2016), 131-37, provides an admirably thorough discussion of the many points of continuity between Dan 9:24-27 and the Olivet Discourse (particularly in Mt 24–25), which all the more should cause readers to note that no mention is made of Jesus as having fulfilled the time predictions of the sixty-nine weeks as the anointed one.

[i]Besides these two occurrences in Dan 9 and the one already mentioned in Is 45, the only use of the term

mashiaḥ in the prophets is Hab 3:13. The references in Psalms often refer to a Davidic king but not necessarily to a future, ideal king.

[i]David E. Aune, *Apocalypticism, Prophecy, and Magic in Early Christianity* (Grand Rapids, MI: Baker Academic, 2008), 19-22. Aune (20) indicates that the earliest apocalypse to include messianic theology is the Similitudes of Enoch.

[k]William Adler, "The Apocalyptic Survey of History Adapted by Christians: Daniel's Prophecy of 70 Weeks," in *The Jewish Apocalyptic Heritage in Early Christianity*, ed. James C. VanderKam and William Adler (Minneapolis: Fortress, 1996), 206-8; and John E. Goldingay, *Daniel*, rev. ed., Word Biblical Commentary 30 (Grand Rapids, MI: Zondervan, 2019), 103.

[l]Starting point 605 BC minus forty-nine years equals 556 BC, roughly when Cyrus ascended the throne of Persia; 597 BC minus forty-nine years equals 548 BC, roughly when Cyrus secured his control of the Medes; 587 BC minus forty-nine years equals 538 BC, when Cyrus issued the proclamation that permitted the Jews to return.

[m]It is common for interpreters to view Dan 11:40-45 as having not been fulfilled in the second century and therefore pointing to a future period and the antichrist. Alternatively, a convincing case can be made that those verses summarize the first two Egyptian campaigns (rather than suggesting a third one) and that the "end" that is referred to (Dan 11:45) is not the death of Antiochus IV Epiphanes but the end of his oppression and the dominion of the Seleucid Empire, which was marked by the Jewish victory at the Battle of Emmaus (between Jerusalem and the sea). Detailed analysis offered in Aubrey E. Buster and John H. Walton, *The Book of Daniel*, New International Commentary on the Old Testament (Grand Rapids, MI: Eerdmans, forthcoming).

[n]George Athas, "In Search of the Seventy 'Weeks' of Daniel 9," *Journal of Hebrew Scriptures* 9 (2009): 13-14, https://jhsonline.org/index.php/jhs/article/view/6231/5259. Also the position adopted in John J. Collins, *Daniel: A Commentary on the Book of Daniel*, Hermeneia (Minneapolis: Fortress, 1994), 355; and Goldingay, *Daniel*, 488. Others have proposed leading figures of the first return, such as Zerubbabel or Sheshbazzar, or even the second return, such as Nehemiah.

[o]For discussion see Adela Yarbro Collins, *Cosmology and Eschatology in Jewish and Christian Apocalypses* (Leiden: Brill, 1996). A work dated to the second century BC, Testament of Levi 16-17, refers to the seventy weeks that the author assumes to be familiar to his readers. The text counts out the seventy weeks as Jubilees and attaches a priest to each one, with the priests referred to as "anointed ones." This shows that in the very period when the book of Daniel found its target audience, the

seventy weeks were connected to the chronography of Jubilee periods and to priests (anointed ones). James L. Kugel, "Testaments of the Twelve Patriarchs," in *Outside the Bible*, ed. Louis H. Feldman, James L. Kugel, and Lawrence H. Schiffman (Philadelphia: Jewish Publication Society, 2013), 2:1697-1855. The Testament of Levi is found in *Outside the Bible* 2:1723-47, and the significant chapters for this discussion are 16-17, *Outside the Bible* 2:1743-45.

[p]For elaboration see Devorah Dimant, "The Seventy Weeks Chronology (Dan. 9, 24-27) in the Light of New Qumranic Texts," in *The Book of Daniel in the Light of New Findings*, ed. A. S. van der Woude (Leuven: Peeters, 1993), 57-76.

[q]Seleucid-era calendar used by the government; Jubilee calendar favored by the Jews. Note Dan 7:25, with the critique that the little horn will "change the set times." For an extensive investigation of this, see Paul J. Kosmin, *Time and Its Adversaries in the Seleucid Empire* (Cambridge, MA: Harvard University Press, 2018).

[r]For extensive investigation and consideration of the various positions and their evidence, see Buster and Walton, *Book of Daniel*, forthcoming.

[s]Haydon, *"Seventy Sevens Are Decreed,"* 146.

[t]Jerome, *Commentary on Daniel* 9.24-27. Jerome presents an extensive summary of interpretations up to and including his time. It stands as a valuable testimony to the varieties of interpretations circulating from the earliest Christian writers. Jerome's commentary is translated by Gleason L. Archer, accessible electronically at www.tertullian.org/fathers/jerome_daniel_02_text.htm.

[u]Katharina Bracht, "The Four Kingdoms of Daniel in Hippolytus's *Commentary on Daniel*," in *Four Kingdom Motifs Before and Beyond the Book of Daniel*, ed. Andrew P. Perrin and Loren T. Stuckenbruck (Leiden: Brill, 2020), 177.

New Testament Apocalyptic Operates by the Same Principles as Old Testament Apocalyptic

Despite some of the qualifications I have been proposing about prophecy and prediction, there should be no doubt that prophecy still has much to tell us about the extension of God's plans and purposes into the future. Nevertheless, instead of talking about promises and timelines, or systems and charts, we should focus on hope and faith. Though no one knows the time, we are to live in expectation of the soon return of Christ. These ideas are most fully developed in the apocalyptic discussion by Jesus in Matthew 24, known as the Olivet Discourse, and in the book of Revelation.

OLIVET DISCOURSE

I must first note that Matthew 24 immediately follows Jesus' lament about Jerusalem (Mt 23:37-39). His disciples encounter him as he leaves the temple, and his initial comments are about the coming destruction of the temple. Jesus' further comments are prompted by the disciples' three questions: When will this happen (presumably the destruction of the temple)? What will be the sign of your coming? And

what will be the sign of the end of the age? Jesus demurs about giving
any specifics of timing (Mt 24:36) and discourages the disciples from
speculating but does indeed give them signs to watch for.

The signs he indicated (Mt 24:4-12) can be easily enumerated: widespread deception, fraudulent claimants, wars, famines, earthquakes,
persecution, oppression, betrayal, attrition, false prophets, and in-
crease of wickedness—basically disruptions of order in every way. The
signs of the end will be the disintegration of order—as happened in
the days of Noah (Mt 24:37). These are all general ways to speak of the
breakdown of order. They are not intended to be a checklist of everything that needs to happen. They are not predictions of the future; they
are recognizable signs of the collapse of both cosmos and civilization.
All of them can be identified in one way or another as happening between the time of this discourse and the destruction of the temple in
AD 70, though also in many ages since.[1]

In Matthew 24:15 Jesus transitions to a specific sign that will occur
amid this breakdown of order, as well as describing the panic that will
unfold in its aftermath. The sign he mentions is the "abomination of
desolation," which he adopts[2] from the book of Daniel and redirects
by giving it a new reference point. The Jews had already experienced
the abomination of desolation in the second-century BC desecration
of the temple by Antiochus IV Epiphanes (Dan 11:31), but here Jesus
adopts the same imagery to refer to the destruction of the temple that
he had described in the opening lines of the chapter. He does not speak
of the coming Roman destruction of the temple as fulfillment of
Daniel. Such adoption and redirection occur when the New Testament
writers pick up topics, themes, ideas, or words from the Old Testament

---

[1]Pointed out by several commentaries; see, for example, Craig S. Keener, *The Gospel of Matthew: A Socio-rhetorical Commentary* (Grand Rapids, MI: Eerdmans, 2009), 569-70.

[2]As noted earlier, in our times this is sometimes called *appropriation*, but *appropriating* is
often perceived negatively, much like *imperialism* or *exploitation*. Using it here would be in
its positive sense, where it refers to adopting a good idea and embracing it, even while
perhaps adapting it to a new situation.

and recontextualize them. I have mentioned that Jesus lays the foundation for this practice in Luke 24. In this sort of use of older texts, repackaging is taking place.[3]

A classic example is found in how many Christians read Job 19:25, "I know that my redeemer lives!" From the classical rendition found in Handel's *Messiah* to more contemporary ones, this affirmation of the work of Christ has been affirmed in music as well as in countless sermons. Nevertheless, when we look carefully at the context in Job, it is clear that his hope is for someone to come along who will take a stand to defend his innocence. He is looking for a "redeemer" who will vindicate him. That is decidedly not Jesus. The redemption provided by Jesus saves us from the wrongs that we did commit; it does not vindicate us, proving our innocence. Yet, I sing the songs as joyously as the next person. As I do so, however, I recognize that I am repackaging the words of Job, not interpreting the message of Job. As discussed extensively above, it is important to recognize the difference between those two, especially when discussing message and fulfillment.[4]

Fulfillment is one form of such repackaging since it is a subcategory used to extend meaning. The redirection of the abomination of desolation by Jesus builds a scenario parallel to that which the Jews had experienced during the terrifying persecution only two centuries earlier. And, as had been the case previously, God's faithful people would become refugees, with all the hazards and threats to survival that such a status brings (Mt 24:15-21). Inconceivably, this time will be even worse than previous persecutions (Mt 24:21). Moreover, as in all times of distress, there will be those who bring false hope (Mt 24:23-28).

---

[3]Consider all the repackaging that can be seen as Peter uses terms such as "God's elect, exiles scattered throughout" (1 Pet 1:1) or "chosen people, a royal priesthood, a holy nation, God's special possession" (1 Pet 2:9), all to describe Gentiles. This is a classic example of repackaging, though it is also building on the ideas already there, not dismissing them.
[4]For more on Job, see John H. Walton and Tremper Longman III, *How to Read Job* (Downers Grove, IL: IVP Academic, 2015), 77-78.

It is only at this point (Mt 24:29) that Jesus invokes a prophetic oracle from the Old Testament as he quotes from Joel 2:10, 31, a classic passage that describes the "day of the LORD." The "day of the LORD" is used in the Old Testament to refer to any time when the ledgers are balanced—the righteous are delivered and elevated while the wicked receive the inevitable consequences of their behavior. The day reflects both God's judgment of the wicked and vindication and deliverance of the righteous. It is not inaccurate to believe that the end of history will be punctuated by a final day of the Lord, but the phrase is also applied to various junctures throughout history.

In such passages, eclipses and other celestial phenomena are used to describe threats to the most fundamental aspects of cosmic order. These are not predictions of specific phenomena that people are to watch for and catalog; they are typical signifiers of the destabilization of order.[5] Here, all of these have been connected by Jesus to the destruction of the temple in Jerusalem at the hand of the Romans—a destruction that was near term. Jesus specifically indicates this with his statement that "this generation will certainly not pass away until all these things have happened" (Mt 24:34).

Finally, this brings us to the "sign of the Son of Man in heaven" (Mt 24:30). Of course, this provides yet another adoption of known terminology, this time from the book of Daniel. In this case, however, it has already been adopted throughout the Gospels so is not new. The imagery of Daniel is continued as the Son of Man comes on the clouds (Dan 7:13). In Daniel he is given authority and glory; here he comes with it (Mt 24:30). Such variations are common when passages are being repackaged. Also characteristic of repackaging, new elements appear: angels sounding the trumpet to gather the elect (Mt 24:31).[6]

---

[5]For discussion of the idea expressed by Jesus and in other New Testament books concerning heaven and earth passing away, see J. Richard Middleton, *A New Heaven and a New Earth: Reclaiming Biblical Eschatology* (Grand Rapids, MI: Baker Academic, 2014), 179-206.

[6]Ideas such as this are connected to the day of the Lord in Joel 2:1 and Zeph 1:16; see Is 27:13 and Zech 9:14.

There is no particular sign given here other than the appearance of Jesus.[7]

BOOK OF REVELATION

Even an Old Testament study of the prophets, such as this current work is, cannot ignore Revelation when addressing eschatology in relation to apocalyptic. Yet, the book of Revelation is not my focus in this book, and I do not have expertise to address it adequately. The literature is massive and widely diverse. Consequently, I can only give a nod to the general direction that I would take. Here I begin with some of the observations of my Old Testament colleague Tremper Longman, as I find his work on genre to be carefully nuanced.[8] He makes two observations that I would like to highlight:

1. Longman speaks of those who try to find modern equivalents to the symbols in the book (for example, locusts as helicopters), noting that such attempts reflect a "faulty belief that the referent can be found at the time of the interpreter."[9] This observation coincides with those that I have already made concerning some of the hazards of identifying what symbols stand for. In apocalyptic, symbols are like the wrapping paper, ribbon, and bow used for a gift. Just as you wouldn't analyze the wrapping paper or the bow and focus on what that tells you about the present inside (although it could), that it is wrapped and has a bow lets us know that what is inside is special. The gift inside is equivalent to the message of prophecy or apocalyptic.[10]

---

[7]Ulrich Luz, *Matthew 21–28* (Minneapolis: Fortress, 2005), 201-2, discusses three interpretations of the sign of the Son of Man: a cross, a banner, or the appearance of the Son of Man himself.
[8]Tremper Longman III, *Revelation Through Old Testament Eyes* (Grand Rapids, MI: Kregel Academic, 2022). Though Longman is an Old Testament scholar rather than an academic who specializes in New Testament in general or the book of Revelation in particular, the approach to Revelation that he adopts, and that I agree with, is adopted by many New Testament scholars as well.
[9]Longman, *Revelation*, 18.
[10]Thanks to Kim Walton for this illustration.

2. He offers an alternative: "It is much more reasonable to understand the analogy in more general terms. These fearful, hybrid locusts stand for horrific devastation that could take many different forms. They could point to war or to environmental devastation or any number of things. The main teaching is that God will bring judgment on sinful humanity."[11]

Longman continues by pointing out that the book of Revelation addresses past, present, and future, just as I have stated about the prophets previously in this book. Clearly, the letters to the seven churches in Revelation address the contemporary circumstances of John. They are experiencing persecution just as the church has often faced throughout its history. That is one of the features that gives the book enduring significance. The call to remain faithful in times of crisis is for all believers of all times and places. Longman points out, however, that not only do the seven letters address John's contemporary audience but the visions do as well. Yet the visions also speak about the future.

The visions have been demonstrated to reflect frequent and creative use of Old Testament material. John, however, is not offering interpretations of, for example, the visions of Daniel, nor is he identifying fulfillments of Ezekiel or Daniel, Isaiah or Zechariah. Instead, as I have mentioned several times in this section, he is adapting material from their visions and reshaping them into his own. This is nowhere clearer than in his reshaping of Daniel's four beasts into a single terrifying beast (Rev 13).[12]

But the question remains, do the visions offer detailed information about the future obscured behind symbols, or, alternatively, do they

[11]Longman, *Revelation*, 18.
[12]I would also agree with those who see John's use of 1,260 days (Rev 11:3; 12:6) as a repackaging that uses numerology linked to the number of the beast rather than as an interpretation of Daniel's "time, times and half a time" (Dan 7:25; 12:7) or as a precise calculation of a future time period. Richard Bauckham, "Nero and the Beast," in *The Climax of Prophecy: Studies in the Book of Revelation* (Edinburgh: T&T Clark, 1993), 400-404.

provide general information about the direction of God's plans and purposes? I agree with Longman as he chooses the latter: "The book does look to the future and indeed to God's final intervention in history to defeat evil and bring his church to himself."[13] This is evident by where the book finds its conclusion—new heaven and new earth, Jesus on the throne, and God dwelling among his people as he had intended since creation.

One of the critical issues when discussing the book of Revelation is the determination of the date of its writing. As with all questions in Revelation, it is complex and highly disputed. Since this current study is not a suitable setting for a full analysis, I can only state that most scholars agree that it was written in the decades after the fall of Jerusalem, and I am going to proceed with that as a given. In this view, the book was written, as most affirm, in the reign of Domitian between AD 80 and 95.[14] That means not only that the temple had already been destroyed but that Nero had come and gone, and the scattering of Jews and Christians throughout the larger region was already taking place in earnest. Persecution, the concept at the heart of Revelation, was widespread in this time, though its intensity varied from one emperor to the next.

Once the premise of this time period is accepted, we are led to conclude that many aspects of Revelation describe events that

---

[13]Longman, *Revelation*, 18. Some who take the first option (detailed information) insist that we need to read the text literally. "Literal" reading, however, requires us to track with the author's rhetorical devices. That is, if he intends a parable, we read the parable as such; if he intends metaphor, we read as metaphor; if he intends symbol, we read as symbol.

[14]This view is almost universally adopted by modern commentators, evangelical or otherwise, confirmed by a quick scan of some of the most prominent ones: Robert H. Mounce, *The Book of Revelation* (Grand Rapids, MI: Eerdmans, 1997), 15-21; David Aune, *Revelation 1–5* (Dallas: Word, 1997), lvii-lxx; G. K. Beale, *The Book of Revelation* (Grand Rapids, MI: Eerdmans, 1999), 4-27; Craig S. Keener, *Revelation* (Grand Rapids, MI: Zondervan, 2000), 35-39; Grant R. Osborne, *Revelation* (Grand Rapids, MI: Baker Academic, 2002), 6-9; Craig R. Koester, *Revelation* (New Haven, CT: Yale University Press, 2014), 71-79; and Francis J. Moloney, *Apocalypse of John: A Commentary* (Grand Rapids, MI: Baker Academic, 2020), 3-4. Aune adopts a two-stage view that sees some of the material as derived from the 60s but with the book itself representing some recalibration completed in the 90s (*Revelation 1–5*, lvii-lviii).

had already taken place in the recent past or were in the process of taking place. For example, it is widely accepted by Revelation scholars that 666 (Rev 13:18) is a cipher for Nero, who died before the destruction of Jerusalem.[15] Nevertheless, that still leaves some future aspects that remain unfulfilled and could feasibly be linchpins for an eschatology.

At this point in my discussion, a word about views of Revelation is in order.[16] Perhaps the most common way that the book is read in churches is designated as "futurist." In this view, the book of Revelation is a chronological map of the end times.[17] A contrasting view considers the future painted as an ideal one (thus, "idealist") that cannot be used to construct a picture of the actual future. A third common view is called the "preterist" view.[18] In this view, the events described in the book are still future to the author but take place in the first century AD (just as a preterist view of Daniel would see the events of that book being fulfilled in the second century BC). To achieve this juxtaposition, preterists often must defend a date for the book of Revelation that predates the fall of Jerusalem.

Without engaging in a detailed analysis of these positions along with their strengths and weaknesses, I simply want to note that none of them are reflected in the approach that I am taking here. Like partial preterists, I accept the premise that the primary sequence of events set forth in Revelation (for example, seals, trumpets, bowls, beasts), apart from the final denouement (for example, resurrection, judgment, new

---

[15]Bauckham, "Nero and the Beast," where he develops a credible case that John is anticipating one like Nero who will arise yet in the future.

[16]Descriptions and comparisons can be found in works such as C. Marvin Pate, ed., *Four Views on the Book of Revelation* (Grand Rapids, MI: Zondervan, 1998).

[17]This view features all the discussions about the rapture, tribulation, and millennium (and differences of opinion in the timing of those events). It includes the viewpoint of dispensationalism.

[18]Two distinct forms of this view are labeled "partial preterism," in which most of the events of the book have taken place in the past, but final events such as the resurrection and the final judgment leading into new heavens and new earth are still future. A contrasting "full preterism" sees all the events of Revelation as having already come about.

heavens and new earth), describes events that took place in the first century AD. In contrast to preterists, however, I believe that many of those passages are encoded descriptions of events that had already taken place, described events that were currently in process, or identified patterns that would find repetition in the future. As such, my view also adopts some aspects of an idealist reading. My agreement is particularly evident in Sam Hamstra's description of his idealist view: "The heart and soul of the idealist approach is that Revelation is an apocalyptic book that presents spiritual precepts through symbols, rather than a book of predictive prophecy fulfilled in specific events or persons in human history."[19] At the same time, such a view would not rule out occasional historical referents, though Hamstra prefers to simply refer to the symbols as "multivalent."[20] Perhaps the view I have adopted fits best into what Keener refers to as an "eclectic" view that combines elements of several positions.[21] In this view, some of the events portrayed in the book have historical referents while others paint a general picture that may be repeated through ages of time. Patterns that may be repeated, often reflected symbolically, are more central than historical events that may be evoked. I have already noted that this is a characteristic of apocalyptic literature.

Coming from a similar direction, Bauckham makes an important observation, with which I heartily agree and which would serve the church well to incorporate into its reading of prophecy and apocalyptic: "Prophecy can only *depict* the future in terms that make sense to its present. It clothes the purpose of God in the hopes and fears of its contemporaries."[22] Bauckham continues,

> John *perceives* the future in the *images* he uses to depict it. It is only as the historical relativity of the images becomes apparent

---

[19]Sam Hamstra Jr., "An Idealist View of Revelation," in Pate, *Four Views*, 129.

[20]Hamstra, "Idealist View of Revelation," 130.

[21]Keener, *Revelation*, 38-39.

[22]Bauckham, "Nero and the Beast," 450, italics his.

to later generations that the impulse to state what the images essentially express arises. Late twentieth-century readers who are serious in their attempt to understand John's prophecy inevitably feel that impulse. But we need to direct it, not into an attempt to replace the images by a supposedly more permanent message, but into an attempt to make the images accessible to ourselves once more. This, after all, is what John himself did with the images of the ancient prophecies of the Old Testament which he was constantly reappropriating for his contemporaries.[23]

In conclusion, I return to the question of what *needs* to happen for prophecy and apocalyptic to be fulfilled. We therefore must take account of the statements of both Jesus and John as they refer to what "must happen" (Mt 24:6; see Rev 1:1). What *must* happen is the kingdom of God must come, and that is all that is needed for prophecy and apocalyptic to find fulfillment. What *will* happen may coincide with observable historical events that follow patterns recognized and recorded in apocalyptic literature, but fulfillment will not fail if certain historical events leading up to the kingdom do not materialize according to some interpreters' expectations. Whatever historical events are referents in the books of Daniel and Revelation have been adequately fulfilled. For Daniel, this includes the four kingdoms, the ten horns, the little horn, and the seventy weeks. For Revelation, it includes nearly everything until the end pages of the book. We may see some of the patterns recycling in future events, but nothing is still needed for the kingdom of God to come. May it come quickly.

---

[23]Bauckham, "Nero and the Beast," 451, italics his.

Concluding Thoughts

A Reading Strategy

Given all that we have discussed throughout this book, how should we read prophetic and apocalyptic texts? What is their role as Scripture? What should characterize our approach? What limitations should we adopt, and what focus will bring the desired result of encountering God in his word?

Barton finds four different approaches to prophecy taken in Second Temple Judaism and the New Testament:[1]

1. as offering ethical models of behavior (in Judaism, known as halakah)[2]

2. as offering predictions of God's ultimate intervention to bring about the end of history and entry into the eschaton[3]

3. as offering secret information into the mysteries of the nature of God (speculative theology)[4]

4. as offering insight into God's plans for human history[5]

---

[1]Introduced and summarized in John Barton, *Oracles of God: Perceptions of Ancient Prophecy in Israel After the Exile* (New York: Oxford University Press, 1986), 152-53.

[2]Described at length in Barton, *Oracles of God*, 154-78.

[3]Described at length in Barton, *Oracles of God*, 179-213.

[4]Described at length in Barton, *Oracles of God*, 235-65.

[5]Described at length in Barton, *Oracles of God*, 214-34.

In Protestant traditions (in my experience at least), the second is perhaps the most popular. Barton offers a reasonable explanation for why this is so:

> In a culture where the continued relevance of holy books is taken for granted, it does not seem far-fetched to see a correspondence between an old prediction (of even a text that was not predictive at all in its original setting) and some contemporary event, and to claim that the ancient prophecy has been "fulfilled."[6]

Barton continues as he explains that the result is a particular inclination that Bible readers find to be natural. "Thus any verse or phrase, taken out of context, might suddenly light up, for someone who knew the text well, because of an incident that seemed to fit so well that it 'must' be what the prophet 'really meant.'"[7] As understandable as this impulse may be, it can pose problems when trying to track with the authors to perceive the authoritative message of the text because such attempts are so often misguided. When that happens, the word of God is brought into disrepute.

In the chapters of this book, I identified some weaknesses in the first three approaches summarized by Barton and made a case for the fourth approach. To make an important differentiation, one can be convinced that God has a grand plan in history and is working it out without believing that we can decipher the details of that plan or that the time we are living in is in fact the culmination of that grand plan (though it may be). In this approach that I have been promoting, prophecy tells us more about the plan and how God has been working it out without the need to identify fulfillment recontextualized for our present ideas or circumstances. I therefore agree with Barton's assessment that this mode of thinking is built on the idea that God, in his wisdom, is in control of history. Consequently, "it is almost a

---

[6]Barton, *Oracles of God*, 192.
[7]Barton, *Oracles of God*, 193.

matter of indifference exactly when the predicted events are to come about."⁸ "*Order* and *pattern* are the crucial elements in all this. It is less important to know what God is going to do and when he will do it then [*sic*] to believe that his actions are regular and purposive and are going somewhere. Past and future often follow patterns."⁹

What does this then require of us when we are reading the prophets? The inclination of many Bible readers today is to encounter the Bible in small chunks. People might be inclined to read a few verses in their morning devotions or to look to an inspirational verse to lift them up or direct them toward God's will. In a Twitter world, we might encounter the word of God in biblical sound bites. Although this approach is not without some benefits, it has resulted in the development of certain assumptions about how Scripture works. That is, we have too readily accepted the idea that each small chunk of Scripture has a spiritual meaning and message of its own—that each narrative, law, psalm, proverb, or prophetic verse carries its own full meaning within itself, waiting to serve the sort of role that some also accord to horoscopes or palm readers. The alternative is to find the meaning in its larger literary and theological context, guided by an understanding of how genres work.

Following this line of thought, I have proposed that, instead of each singular piece of Scripture being viewed as a personalized message to my life and circumstances, each of those pieces has a contribution to make to my understanding of the plans and purposes of God.¹⁰ In this approach, the significance of each singular piece is not found in "what it means to me" but in what it says about God. It is part of God's story. Its meaningfulness to each one of us is that it contributes to our understanding of the plans and purposes of God as we seek, moment by

---

⁸Barton, *Oracles of God*, 224.

⁹Barton, *Oracles of God*, 225-26 (italics his).

¹⁰For more complete discussion, see John H. Walton, *Wisdom for Faithful Reading* (Downers Grove, IL: IVP Academic, 2023), chap. 37.

moment, to be active, engaged, committed participants in his kingdom plans and purposes.

I have argued elsewhere that it is not the Bible's objective to provide a comprehensive system of morals or theology, though at times its content is pertinent to both.[11] The Bible is not trying to direct us to the will of God for making the important decisions of life (who to marry, what job to take, what vocation to pursue). It is not recounting history or unfolding science. And it is not encoded to tell the future. It is God's revelation about what he has done and continues to do in the world. As we learn his story, we get to know him more deeply and can improve our commitment and ability to work alongside him as he does his work in us and through us. The idea that prophecy provides an understanding of God's work in history from beginning to end provides what Barton calls a "spiritual foundation"; that is, "knowing what God is set on achieving in the world, one can fit oneself better to his plans."[12]

UNDERSTANDING THE CONTEMPORARY SIGNIFICANCE OF THE PROPHETIC MESSAGES

If prophecy, as I have maintained, is so inextricably connected to covenant, what does that say about the significance of Israelite prophecy to those outside the covenant? The prophetic understanding of the divine plan was associated with the covenant, not with the wide scope of history or the eschatological age to come (though some of that is picked up in apocalyptic literature). Consequently, when we want to find the application and relevance of the prophets to our own lives, we should not look to fulfillment or eschatology. Instead, we ought to engage the prophets at the level of their *messages*. As I described earlier in the book, those messages consistently pertain to indictment,

---

[11]John H. Walton and J. Harvey Walton, *The Lost World of the Torah* (Downers Grove, IL: IVP Academic, 2019).
[12]Barton, *Oracles of God*, 227-28.

judgment, instruction, and aftermath. Here we can briefly address each in turn.

Indictment. What does God care about? If we desire to be in relationship with God, things that matter to him should matter to us. To give the sentiment a poetic turn, we should want to be able to see into the heart of God. That is what prophetic literature allows us to do. We are not Israel, and we may or may not be guilty of the same sins as Israel, though we may find that we could be guilty of the same *kinds* of sins. When we read the indictments that God prompted the prophets to deliver to Israel, we should respond by thinking about how we might also be guilty of similar offenses. Are we pursuing justice, or are we neglecting or oppressing those who are disadvantaged? Are our worship practices focused on trying to manipulate God to oblige him to shower us with blessings? Justice and worship were two of the areas in which Israel was failing miserably, and we struggle with the same issues. God cares about justice for the defenseless, and so should we. God cares about the integrity of worship, so we should guard it. Unfaithfulness in our lives is deeply disappointing to God, who has done so much for us, just as he had done much for Israel.

The prophets' indictments also focused on misplaced alliances as the Israelites depended on their political and social strategies instead of depending on God. Today it might be the political parties that we align with or the social agendas that we adopt. Perhaps it is the organizations in which we participate or the strategies into which we pour our energy. In these we are not unlike the Israelites.

The Israelites suffered from confused priorities, and we are no different. Social status, wealth, power, popularity, and prestige are easy to prioritize. We are in the pursuit of happiness, and we desire to flourish—no surprise, these are natural impulses. But what priority should these have in our lives? The indictments of the prophets confronted Israelites with all these challenges. When we read the prophets, we should be examining our own lives and attitudes to determine whether we care about the same things that God cares about.

Judgment. The prophets also give a lot of attention to judgment. When we read the prophets, we must move beyond the descriptions of judgment that the Israelites had pronounced on them, or even the judgments that came about. The judgments pronounced and executed on Israel again show us the heart of God, but not in the ways that people often perceive it in the Old Testament. These judgment oracles do not proclaim that God is an angry, punishing God who takes offense at the slightest deviation. They show a God who has been faithful and gracious for centuries in the face of blatant, disrespectful, insulting unfaithfulness. Yet, he cannot be scorned indefinitely; he is not to be trifled with. If there is to be order and justice in the world, there must be accountability and consequences.

It is interesting that these days some people turn away from Christianity because they say they cannot believe in a God who would allow the injustice and suffering in the world that is evident all around us. Yet some of those same people will read the Old Testament and decry the God who brings judgment. We can't have it both ways!

The judgment oracles of the Old Testament convince us that God is serious about faithfulness and justice. His patience and grace are extended far beyond measure, but the time comes when judgment is necessary. This should serve as a warning to us as individuals, to our nation, and to the church: we are accountable to a holy God.

Instruction. The instruction we find in the prophets is oriented to the covenant to which we are not party, but that does not make it irrelevant to us. The prophets called on God's people to repent, to turn from their wicked ways, to be faithful, to worship with integrity, to do justice—all behaviors that the covenant promoted. These continue to be what God wants from his people. Israel had the covenant with its *tôrâ*, which told them how to pursue order in their relationship with God. Christians today are not under that covenant and never were, but we have the example and teaching of Christ that leads us to right living, pleasing to God.

We are not without instruction; we know what God wants of us. As in Israel of old, God wants his people today to bring honor to his name. As with Israel in the Old Testament, God has chosen us as his; he has identified himself with us, and we should identify with him. We should be working to bring about his kingdom on earth (not ours) and doing his will (not ours). We should be working toward establishing his order, not our own, and participating in his plans and purposes rather than pursuing our own benefits. These principles are what the prophets teach, and they should be prioritized over engaging in arguments about the timing of the rapture.

Aftermath. I have been contending for the idea that aftermath oracles are not intended to inform us of the details of the future. They give messages of hope, and we need that today as much as the Israelites did. Otherwise, it would be easy to fall into despair. We trust that God has time and history in his hand and that, in the end, the father of time is a prince of peace (Is 9:6). In Jeremiah 29:11 the prophet was telling his Israelite audience that God had a hope and a future for them. Even though that is not a promise made to us, we believe that we can have hope because the future is going to unfold according to God's plans and purposes. The future is God's kingdom.

All of this helps us to realize that God's word for us through the prophets is bound in the message of the prophets, not in how those messages found fulfillment or might yet do so. We still stand in need of hearing the messages of the prophets and being convicted, warned, guided, or encouraged by them. The people of Israel were supposed to respond to the messages of the prophets, and no less is expected of us when we encounter those messages. Our circumstances are not the same as those in Israel, but God still wants his people today to respond, even as we face our own human failings, which are not that different from Israel's. The call to respond was inherent even in the prophetic oracles given to the kings in the ancient Near East. Even the gods of the Babylonians wanted the hearing audience to respond. Being responsive to God is at the heart of prophecy.

THINKING ABOUT FULFILLMENT TODAY

We should not consider the prophetic oracles of the Old Testament to be arcane or opaque. They very clearly testify to the plans and purposes of God being worked out on the canvas of history—and that is what we are to observe and from which we are to learn. All of this is found in the *messages* of the prophets, which are largely transparent to any reader. In contrast, *fulfillment* is heaven's business.

We have clear indication that fulfillment has happened in the past. The New Testament writers are deeply invested in making that point, one that is affirmed repeatedly by Jesus. We embrace such evidences as we connect the dots from the prophets to the Gospels and see God's plans coming to fruition. Furthermore, we should have no doubt that fulfillment will continue to unfold as God's plans and purposes proceed on his time schedule. Confidence in continuing fulfillment, however, is not the same as confidence in our ability to determine what those fulfillments will look like or when and how they will take place. A strong case can be made that Paul was of the opinion that Jesus would return in his lifetime, and it is easy to imagine that Jesus' words could have easily been taken that way. When he talked about the return of the Son of Man with his angels to reward people for their deeds, he stated that some standing there would not see death before the arrival of the Son of Man and his kingdom (Mt 16:27-28). Though some may have therefore expected the return of Jesus within that generation, fulfillment did not unfold in the expected ways.

How should we react when we, or others, see events unfolding before us that look like they could be fulfillments of prophetic oracles or apocalyptic visions? We should respond with patience and reserve. Nothing is to be gained by advancing such connections between modern events and prophecy. We trust that God is at work, and we live in hope of the return of Christ and the culmination of his plans and purposes in his kingdom come. Whether we have identified signs correctly or connected dots appropriately changes nothing. We live as his people giving honor to his name and testimony to his work in our lives regardless.

When we see what we interpret to be signs of the kingdom's arrival, our hope may be fanned into flame, but we should not need such signs to be fervent in hope. Here are some important insights that can guide how we think:

- Hold our imaginations at bay. We dare not position ourselves as the arbiters of God's plans and purposes.

- Focus on what has authority in Scripture. It is only that authority that embodies the significance of Scripture for us as God's people.

- Be responsive to God in our lives, whether the end is nigh or not. The prophets and visionaries of the Old Testament spoke the word of God in order to prompt response, and God's people throughout time should read those words considering what sort of people they should be.

- Resist trying to decipher current events in light of prophecy. Humility is key.

- Humbly submit to Jesus' repeated insistence that no one knows the time. It should be transparent to us that we should not try to do that which Jesus tells us we should not and cannot do.

All well and good, one might say, but didn't Jesus expect his audience to recognize the signs and acknowledge that he was the fulfillment? He appears to condemn the Pharisees for their blindness to how he was the fruition of God's plan as laid out in the Old Testament. A fair point, but let's think through what he expected of them.

Jesus criticizes the Jewish leaders by observing that "you know how to interpret the appearance of the sky, but you cannot interpret the signs of the times" (Mt 16:3). This statement of Jesus occurs only here in the New Testament and, as R. T. France observes, has often been connected to eschatological expectation. He disagrees with that, indicating that "the reference is not to future events but to what is already there for all to see. . . . They ought to be able to see that important events are taking place, that this is the time of decision."[13] Craig Keener takes this to the next step, suggesting the sinfulness of the current generation itself should have been the sign that was recognized because it was widely believed that a sinful generation would precede the kingdom of God.[14] In contrast, Jesus never suggests that they should have figured out Daniel's seventy weeks. Calamitous signs referred to in the Olivet Discourse serve to alert people and remind them to be aware that the disasters they experience are not the end, but such events will usher in the kingdom of God.

Jesus *performed* signs and expected his audience to recognize them as indicative that he had come from God. He affirmed that everything must be fulfilled, but he did not tell them how or when. Notice that in the list of woes to the Pharisees (Mt 23), the failure to recognize prophetic signs is not among them.

LIVING IN THE END TIMES
(EVERYONE BELIEVES THEY ARE, AND THAT IS OKAY)

Apocalyptic conditions since the earliest literature featured the collapse of order in two primary arenas: the human and the cosmic. Concern for collapse in the human arena focused on destructive warfare. Collapse in the cosmic arena featured natural disasters: drought, famine, plague, earthquakes, floods, locusts, and so on. Beginning in the mid-twentieth century, the world faced warfare on a scale never before imagined, coupled with the development of weaponry that

---

[13]R. T. France, *The Gospel of Matthew* (Grand Rapids, MI: Eerdmans, 2007), 606.
[14]Craig S. Keener, *The Gospel of Matthew: A Socio-rhetorical Commentary* (Grand Rapids, MI: Eerdmans, 2009), 421.

could wreak destruction at unprecedented levels. Fear found new terrifying scenarios that fragile international politics fed regularly. Now jeopardy and danger are likewise pervasive on the local level as shooters infiltrate our schools with violence.

While threat of war that reaches all corners of the globe remains a far too realistic scenario, many today still only observe from the outside the wars that others are experiencing. As outside observers, war in our region, while always a possibility, seems not to pose immediate threat. Those experiencing war in their region, however, may well believe they are living in the end times.

Collapse in the cosmic arena has likewise reached new heights. Famine and drought are not new and have always been experienced regionally or in cycles. Destruction caused by cosmic catastrophes has been documented throughout human history, their horror unabated. And, as if the list of cosmic threats were somehow yet deficient, humans themselves have, at times inadvertently, become agents in cosmic collapse, which goes by the milder name of climate change.

Perhaps today we find our closest comparison to Old Testament prophecies of impending warfare in the statistics and physical evidence of climate change. Climate-change projections include the depletion of the ozone layer, melting of the ice caps, weather patterns that are more violent and less predictable, rising sea levels, biodiversity loss, species extinctions, famine caused by loss of food production areas, disappearance of rain forests, CO_2 issues, fossil fuel dependence, and more. These may be compared to the prophetic projections of invasion, destruction of cities and temple, exile, and so on.

In our modern context, those with specialized knowledge (from science rather than from God) also warn about impending doom—now, however, in the collapse of the ecosystem as a result of climate change to which we ourselves have contributed. These specialists paint a picture of a disastrous future, auguring a world very different from the one we enjoy today. Their prognostications are sometimes more general, other times fairly specific, but, as I have claimed regarding the Old Testament prophets and visionaries, they are not predicting the future.

Unlike the prophets, however, these specialists are not projecting either divine plans and purposes, or any human designs. Nevertheless, they speak of what they believe will be the inevitable result of our present course of action, as the prophets did. They speak of consequences—consequences that may yet be avoided *if we take steps in the present*. In that sense, like classical prophecy, they address the present with a cautionary message built on a vision of an undesirable future.

It is not my intention to turn this into a manifesto for creation care. Others have done that far more ably than I could.[15] Instead, I would like to highlight similarities and differences to compare a contemporary situation to the ancient one that we have been studying. First, I will consider key points of similarity between the messages of the prophets/visionaries of the Old Testament and the scientists and culture watchers who are challenging us about climate change today.

- The respective specialists, both Old Testament and current, are projecting present behavior into future consequences.

- The primary focus is not to tell the future but to warn the current generation in order to change behavior.

- Both sets of specialists have messages of indictment, judgment (consequences), and instruction.[16]

---

[15]See for example, Douglas J. Moo and Jonathan A. Moo, *Creation Care: A Biblical Theology of the Natural World* (Grand Rapids, MI: Zondervan, 2018); and Sandra L. Richter, *Stewards of Eden: What Scripture Says About the Environment and Why It Matters* (Downers Grove, IL: IVP Academic, 2020).

[16]It is interesting that some specialists today warn that the solutions are not just scientific ones but spiritual ones. Gus Speth was the founder and former president of the World Resources Institute. He was a co-founder of the Natural Resources Defense Council, a senior adviser to Presidents Jimmy Carter and Bill Clinton, professor of law at Georgetown University, administrator of the United Nations Development Program, and, for a time, dean of the Yale School of Forestry and Environmental Studies. In a widely quoted interview on BBC's *Shared Planet* in 2013, Speth made the following amazing statement:

- Warnings are intended to impress their present audience with the severity of future consequences (doomsday scenarios) for present behavior.

- There are similarities in the degree of specificity, both in terms of what is expected and when it might come upon us.

- Specialists can be found to support different perspectives.

- National leaders often express skepticism about the reality of the threat.

- It is difficult to motivate people to believe and change.

- Both present the possibility that the consequences can be averted if change takes place in the present.

- Small steps in the right direction may slow or postpone the anticipated consequences.

At the same time, it is also important to highlight significant differences. Specifically, modern discussions about climate change are not characterized by certain features that were distinctives of classical prophecy and apocalyptic.

- Modern warnings are not generally considered a message from God.

- No aftermath is cited regarding the horrors associated with ecosystem collapse. Modern specialists offer no hope for recovery after the collapse. Humans can exacerbate the problem or, alternatively, do what they can to bring improvement and better prospects, but only God can restore or re-create order.

- Nothing in the modern conversation is connected to covenant.

"I used to think that the top environmental problems were biodiversity loss, ecosystem collapse, and climate change. I thought that thirty years of good science could address these problems. I was wrong. The top environmental problems are selfishness, greed, and apathy, and to deal with these we need a cultural and spiritual transformation. And we scientists don't know how to do that."

- Modern danger is presented not as judgment from God but as the inevitable consequence of destructive human industry.

- No connection is made between the threat and God's plans and purposes.

We might also compare the ancient Israelite scenario with our own modern one in terms of response. There are those of us who believe the science and take the threats associated with climate change seriously. Yet, how much do we actually do? Maybe we recycle, try to drive less, and reduce our carbon footprint. We think about ways to "go green," patronize companies that are conscientious about the environment, and maybe even make donations to organizations trying to do something about it. But perhaps we have not gone so far as to put solar panels on our houses or buy an electric car. For many of us, our attempts are haphazard and maybe even half-hearted as we wonder whether the little that we do as individuals can really make a difference. Such half-hearted responses can be compared to those of the Israelites, who believed the prophets and tried to consider how they could respond but still came up short. Sometimes it might have been difficult to see what behaviors needed to change.

I have developed this comparison to help us consider the question, Are we living in the last days? We may well be, but maybe not. Not a very satisfying response, is it? Nevertheless, I stand by it. The specialists of our day—whether climate-change scientists, politicians commenting on the threat of war, or theologians discussing the collapse of formal religion and the church—can only evaluate the signs and warn of possible consequences. The classical prophets did the same.

Just like the Israelites, we have not been given sure knowledge of a specific future. The warnings we receive, however, should be sufficient for us to respond by doing what we can to change direction. At the same time, we trust that God's plans and purposes are being effectuated even in the troubled, at times devastating, crises in which we live. Even in desperate times, fatalism is not the answer, nor is an attitude of neglect, adopting the attitude that the world going to rack and ruin will accelerate the coming of God's kingdom. We should not continue in sin that grace may abound. We should likewise recognize that all our attempts to decode prophecy and apocalyptic to gain certain knowledge of the future are a vanity we cannot afford to indulge.

The future is in God's hands, and in him we trust, not in our calculations and timelines. We should live as if we are in the end times, as uncounted generations have also believed. Such conviction calls on us to respond responsibly to the current crisis and to trust God's wisdom and timing.

For Further Reading

Archer, Gleason, Jr., and Gregory C. Chirichigno. *Old Testament Quotations in the New Testament: A Complete Survey.* Chicago: Moody, 1983.

Aune, David E. *Prophecy in Early Christianity and the Ancient Mediterranean World.* Grand Rapids, MI: Eerdmans, 1983.

Barton, John. *Oracles of God: Perceptions of Ancient Prophecy in Israel After the Exile.* New York: Oxford University Press, 1986.

Bauckham, Richard. *The Climax of Prophecy: Studies on the Book of Revelation.* Edinburgh: T&T Clark, 1993.

Beale, G. K., ed. *The Right Doctrine from the Wrong Texts?: Essays on the Use of the Old Testament in the New.* Grand Rapids, MI: Baker Books, 1994.

Beale, G. K., and D. A. Carson, eds. *Commentary on the New Testament Use of the Old Testament.* Grand Rapids, MI: Baker Academic, 2007.

Ben Zvi, Ehud, and Michael H. Floyd, eds. *Writings and Speech in Israelite and Ancient Near Eastern Prophecy.* Atlanta: Society of Biblical Literature, 2000.

Boda, Mark J., and Lissa M. Wray Beal. *Prophets, Prophecy, and Ancient Israelite Historiography.* Winona Lake, IN: Eisenbrauns, 2013.

Chalmers, Aaron. *Interpreting the Prophets.* Downers Grove, IL: IVP Academic, 2015.

Collins, John J. *Apocalypticism in the Dead Sea Scrolls.* New York: Routledge, 1997.

———, ed. *The Oxford Handbook of Apocalyptic Literature*. New York: Oxford University Press, 2014.

Ellis, Maria deJong. "Observations on Mesopotamian Oracles and Prophetic Texts." *Journal of Cuneiform Studies* 41, no. 2 (1989): 127-86.

Gonzalez, Hervé. "No Prophetic Texts from the Hellenistic Period?" Pages 294-340 in *Times of Transition: Judea in the Early Hellenistic Period*, edited by Sylvie Honigman, Christophe Nihan, and Oded Lipschits. University Park, PA: Eisenbrauns, 2021.[1]

Gordon, Robert P., and Hans M. Barstad, eds. *"Thus Speaks Ishtar of Arbela": Prophecy in Israel, Assyria, and Egypt in the Neo-Assyrian Period*. Winona Lake, IN: Eisenbrauns, 2013.

Guinan, Ann Kessler. "A Severed Head Laughed: Stories of Divinatory Interpretation." Pages 7-40 in *Magic and Divination in the Ancient World*, edited by Leda Ciraolo and Jonathan Seidel. Ancient Magic and Divination 2. Leiden: Brill/Styx, 2002.

Hamori, Esther J. *Women's Divination in Biblical Literature*. New Haven, CT: Yale University Press, 2015.

Koch, Klaus. *The Prophets*. Vol. 1, *The Assyrian Period*. Philadelphia: Fortress, 1982.

———. *The Prophets*. Vol. 2, *The Babylonian and Persian Periods*. Philadelphia: Fortress, 1982.

Koch, Ulla Susanne. *Mesopotamian Divination Texts: Conversing with the Gods*. Münster: Ugarit-Verlag, 2015.

Lenzi, Alan, and Jonathan Stökl, eds. *Divination, Politics, and Ancient Near Eastern Empires*. Atlanta: Society of Biblical Literature, 2014.

Lindblom, Johannes. *Prophecy in Ancient Israel*. Philadelphia: Fortress, 1962.

Longenecker, Richard N. *Biblical Exegesis in the Apostolic Period*. Grand Rapids, MI: Eerdmans, 1975.

Longman, Tremper, III. *Revelation Through Old Testament Eyes*. Grand Rapids, MI: Kregel, 2022.

---

[1] Interesting discussion of prophetic books being reworked and supplemented in the Hellenistic period; see especially the summary conclusion on 316-17 and *Fortschreibungen* on 298 (added sections intentionally imitated the books that they were supplementing).

Maul, Stefan M. *The Art of Divination in the Ancient Near East: Reading the Signs of Heaven and Earth*. Translated by Brian McNeil and Alexander Johannes Edmonds. Waco, TX: Baylor University Press, 2018.

Middleton, J. Richard. *A New Heaven and a New Earth: Reclaiming Biblical Eschatology*. Grand Rapids, MI: Baker Academic, 2014.

Nissinen, Martti. *Ancient Prophecy: Near Eastern, Biblical, and Greek Perspectives*. Oxford: Oxford University Press, 2017.

———. *Prophecy in Its Ancient Near Eastern Context*. Atlanta: Society of Biblical Literature, 2000.

———. *Prophets and Prophecy in the Ancient Near East*. With contributions by C. L. Seow, Robert K. Ritner, and H. Craig Melchert. 2nd ed. Atlanta: Society of Biblical Literature, 2019.

Nogalski, James D., and Marvin A. Sweeney, eds. *Reading and Hearing the Book of the Twelve*. Atlanta: Society of Biblical Literature, 2000.

Parpola, Simo. *Assyrian Prophecies*. State Archives of Assyria 9. Helsinki: Helsinki University Press, 1997.

Portier-Young, Anathea. *Apocalypse Against Empire*. Grand Rapids, MI: Eerdmans, 2011.

Sharp, Caroline, ed. *The Oxford Handbook of the Prophets*. New York: Oxford University Press, 2016.

Stökl, Jonathan. *Prophecy in the Ancient Near East*. Leiden: Brill, 2012.

Westermann, Claus. *Basic Forms of Prophetic Speech*. Translated by Hugh Clayton White. 1967. Reprint, Louisville, KY: Westminster John Knox, 1991.

———. *Prophetic Oracles of Salvation in the Old Testament*. Translated by Keith Crim from the 1987 German edition. Louisville, KY: Westminster John Knox, 1991.

Wilson, Robert R. *Prophecy and Society in Ancient Israel*. Philadelphia: Fortress, 1980.

Wright, N. T. *Surprised by Hope*. New York: HarperOne, 2008.

Yarbro Collins, Adela. *Cosmology and Eschatology in Jewish and Christian Apocalypticism*. Leiden: Brill, 1996.

General Index

Scripture Index

Scripture Index
183

1 Peter
1:1, *150*
1:10-11, *122*
1:10-12, *63*
1:12, *123*

2:9, *150*
2:22, *93*

2 Peter
1:20-21, *101*
1:21, *75*

Revelation
1, *132*
1–5, *154*
1:1, *157*
11:3, *153*
12:6, *153*

13, *153*
13:18, *137, 155*
14, *136*
17, *136*
19, *136*

The Lost World Series

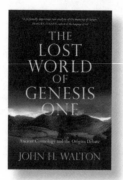

The Lost World of Genesis One
978-0-8308-3704-5

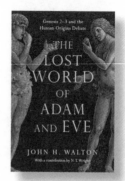

The Lost World of Adam and Eve
978-0-8308-2461-8

The Lost World of the
Israelite Conquest
978-0-8308-5184-3

The Lost World of Scripture
978-0-8308-4032-8

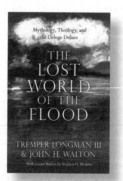

The Lost World of the Flood
978-0-8308-5200-0